KARMA S

Rajendar Menen is a senior journalist who has been published in several countries. He began his career with *The Times of India* in Mumbai. He has launched and edited magazines, written four books on different aspects of healing, and freelanced for organizations such as the BBC, UNFPA, France 2, Gulf News, Ray of Hope, and Teacher's Training Centre, Tralee, Ireland. He has co-authored books on AIDS and prostitution in South Asia, and edited three journals on the technical and human aspects of HIV/AIDS. The street is his muse. He lives and works in Mumbai.

KARMA SUTRA

ADVENTURES OF A STREET BUM

Rajendar Menen

HarperCollins *Publishers* India
a joint venture with

New Delhi

First published in India in 2012 by
HarperCollins *Publishers* India
a joint venture with
The India Today Group

Copyright © Rajendar Menen 2012

An earlier version was first published in 2007 by Saga Books in Canada

ISBN: 978-93-5029-094-1

2 4 6 8 10 9 7 5 3 1

Rajendar Menen asserts the moral
right to be identified as the author of this work.

HarperCollins *Publishers*
A-53, Sector 57, Noida 201301, India
77-85 Fulham Palace Road, London W6 8JB, United Kingdom
Hazelton Lanes, 55 Avenue Road, Suite 2900, Toronto, Ontario M5R 3L2
and 1995 Markham Road, Scarborough, Ontario M1B 5M8, Canada
25 Ryde Road, Pymble, Sydney, NSW 2073, Australia
31 View Road, Glenfield, Auckland 10, New Zealand
10 East 53rd Street, New York NY 10022, USA

Typeset in ITC Giovanni Std 10.5/14
InoSoft Systems Noida

Printed and bound at
Thomson Press (India) Ltd.

For Dom, who told me to write.

For 'Wanda Woman', who liberated me from bondage.

For Anna and the angels, who followed me everywhere and kept me in one piece.

For Ruby, who is a gem.

For Maree Agland, who made *Karma Sutra* happen.

For *The Daily*, for pioneering street reportage.

For all those who lived and died along the way. My dharma buddies. So many of you.

Finally, for the sex workers of the world. Without them, this planet would be such a small place!

Contents

Preface

Perhaps the only thing more difficult than to be indifferent to India would be to describe or understand India completely.
—'A Rough Guide to India'

I have been on the street most of my life. I am still on the street.

It's been a deliberate decision. A choice I have made in my saner moments. It's the only way to understand the magical mosaic of the Indian street.

I love the excitement of disorder that the street exhibits with such vivid imagination. The colours, sounds, smells and dangers send the adrenaline pounding. There is never a dull moment. You live with the unexpected. You court it without fear. You wander with the flow and go where it takes you. It never lets you down. It is startling, irreverent, exciting, agonizing, desperate, raw, even tragic.

The book is not backed by ideology or dogma. It is not political. It is without prejudice or bias. No insult is intended. No individual, social group, community, caste or religion is targeted. All names have been changed where necessary and all identities protected. It is not about activism or intended reform. No state secrets have been compromised. It is not a definitive document on the street. If anything, it is about empirical evidence and gut-level reaction. There are several colours on the street. I have tried to absorb some of them.

The book doesn't wear any moral garb. It is not judgemental.
It doesn't tell you how to live, or how not to live. It just tells you
how it is. If I have made statements, they are a reaction to how the
street has impacted me. It is my opinion, straight from the heart.
Not sponsored or designed by an outside agency.

I have deliberately avoided statistics. I have also gone out of
my way to not quote anyone in the government. Figures can be
doctored and interpreted either way convincingly, and we all know
the answers of those in power.

This book is mainly about my experiences on the streets of
Mumbai, one of the greatest cities of the world. It is about the
darkness on the streets. It's about the lives of the marginalized,
and their heroic battle against the enormous odds stacked against
them every single day of their lives. It is about how they surmount
it all without complaint: the true heroes of a karma that has
shackled them.

It is about sex workers, drug addicts, hijras, Devadasis, the
homeless and the dying, and the hundreds of thousands of people
who wander into India's most glamorous city to seek the crumbs.
It is about the other side of midnight in a city that is also equally
gross about its display of power and pelf.

I have crossed the boulevard, lived with those who inhabit it,
and broken bread with them. I have had the option of returning
to my life of comfort when I wanted to. So it has been easy. But
those on the streets were condemned to their fate. For them, there
was no escape. It takes great skill, wit and cunning on their part to
get out of it unscathed. This book documents their sutra; the sutra
that extracts every inch of guile to help them battle their karma.

The street is a living entity, its code well outside the pale of
normally accepted behaviour. When you are in the trenches
every day of your life, and survival is etched on your mind as
your primary goal, you make your own rules. It is often not in
consonance with what those who make the laws have in mind.

Circumstances give birth to protest, revolt and rebellion. Anarchy has its seeds in misfortune, whether real or perceived. It is difficult to understand this pain or its expression if you are not of the street. It is also easy to exploit it and use it to advantage.

The police are let out on the mean streets to look after them. They have it rough. They are poorly paid, desperately outnumbered, manipulated by their political masters, and low on morale. But they are in constant touch with the marginalized. They are human, too, and get to see all sides of the dice. It works on them. They see the corruption and the loopholes in the law, and exploit it. They can become a terrifying presence.

The research for the book took several years, from the 1980s to the late 1990s. During the period, the city also changed its name from Bombay to Mumbai. There have been cosmetic changes to other locations too. This book is not a chronology of events. There are no specific dates. Situations may have changed but the flavour of the street will remain for a long time.

Most of the interviews were in Hindi. I have cut out the profanity from the street dialect to give it to you in as acceptable a form as possible. I have also tried to look at things with a sense of humour to soften the blow.

I have been fortunate to have been on this ride. Join me.

1 December 2011   Rajendar Menen

UNTOLD CHRONICLES

There is a field beyond all notions of right and wrong. Come, meet me there.

—Rumi

I have been interviewing commercial sex workers and others who live on – and off – the street for over two decades. I shall begin with the sex worker before moving on to the others.

In the good old days the sex worker was simply known as a prostitute. A word short and straight, like a powerful upper cut. No frills, no ornamentation. It takes you to the count in a swift jab.

Then the world got politically correct. You couldn't call someone short or fat or dark or thin anymore. It wasn't polite. They were all suitably and substantially 'challenged'. The compassion extended to the prostitute too. Wise minds sat together and decided that even if nothing could be done about the job portfolio, the practitioner could be rewarded with a title that looked good on a visiting card. How could somebody be called a prostitute in the days of McDonalds and Microsoft? And what was the point in meeting at exotic locales all over the world at great cost and debating the merits of prostitution endlessly if nothing could be done for the prostitute? So the poor woman (we are gender-specific here) could now die of AIDS and tell the accusing world till her last breath that she wasn't a prostitute but a commercial sex worker. It was a grand title. She could die in peace. Her epitaph would read well.

As a rookie in one of the biggest newspapers in the world, I had several beats to choose from. It was always easy to sit in an opulent patisserie and take down notes, return to the office and file a report. I did this for a while and got scared. What if I got fattened by the food, drink and the junkets and died of cardiac arrest in a supersonic jet across the Pacific en route to the inauguration of a new fleet of airplanes? It wouldn't be as exciting as a bullet grazing my nape in a bunker. A confession: I am an excitement junkie. I like to waste my life, rather than do nothing with it. I have lived recklessly – spending time and money on the street – and given myself to what Osho called the care of 'existence ', which simply meant surrender to a higher force. That was good advice. I am still in one piece.

Each one of us is born to forces beyond our control. I was born into a middle-class milieu, to a confluence of circumstances that ensured a fairly easy life for me. I was born into a family that believed in quality education and to a code of values that incorporated integrity and hard work. Opportunities would come knocking and I would have the luxury of choice. This simple accident of birth determines the course of one's life in the 'developing' world. But somewhere along the way, I decided to hew my own path and march to a different drumbeat.

I met Radha in my late teens. She was slightly older than me but I was told that she could love a man with the force of a hurricane at level six. She even insisted that I take the only gold chain that she had. She owned nothing of material consequence but wanted the best for me. This gesture had me stumped. This wasn't middle class. She was a prostitute, had already slept with many men and had plumbed the depths of loss and despair within years of sighting adulthood. And here she was gifting me a valuable ornament that she had really worked hard for. And who was I? Nothing more special than a clean-faced youth who had befriended her. But she took her chance. She lived dangerously. I liked that. We were kindred spirits. My first interview, I think, began with her.

Over the years, I went on to interview thousands of sex workers. I have launched and edited journals on HIV/AIDS, written books and countless articles on the subject and been part of several television teams from all over the world keen on documenting on camera their strange zone of existence. The sex worker is fascinating – her life so different from ours – but intimidating, too.

There is a huge moral streak running down the pants of society and she sends a tremor through it. You mention the word 'prostitute' and there is excitement, there is vicarious interest, many eager questions are asked in hushed tones, and a lot will be said behind your back. The majority wants nothing to do with you. Their world-view, built with ordinary self-righteousness, gets a knock on the head. You are a bad man even for talking about her world with some enthusiasm. But who visits the sex worker? Why she has been in existence for so long? Who fuels her demand? Who else but the proselytising moral brigade walking bowlegged between desire and duty and unable to fulfil either.

I have visited brothels in different parts of the world. I have sampled the street and the bougainvillea that shadows it. I have known the high and mighty who can't live without the sex worker and also those kicked in the butt by life but still glued to her eyelashes. Art, cinema and literature pay tribute to the courtesan. She has an indisputable place in the history of nations, and is the heroine of several mythologies that have helped structure

3

the feathers of modern society. Love and, possibly, its sexual expression, gives mortal existence a new lease of hope. It gives life to deadend situations. It helps you dream, fantasize, fly. In the everyday existence of salaries, bills, taxes, rearing families, ill-health, old age, pensions, insurance claims, debt and finally, death, escape routes are vital for sanity. The escape hatch depends on temperament, attitude, personality, circumstances, religious beliefs, conscience, genetics, disposable income and several other ingredients.

The sex worker is feared. She is condemned because she can break the delicately woven fabric of society. Accept her as an integral part of life, and the family can be ruined. She is a threat to middle-class institutions that make room for progeny, the sharing of property and the continuity, in some order, of the human race. Gender harmony is tenuous at the best of times. Why give it another handle to usher a faster collapse? Man is anarchic deep within. Validating the sex worker and her hold on you will result in social chaos. Sexually transmitted diseases have added to her public ostracism.

It is the era of AIDS. Society has become permissive, there is sex for the asking, birth control is easy, and yet the sex worker is in greater demand than ever before. Surely, there has to be a good reason for this flagrant violation of simple logic and the umbrella of morality that is foisted on society.

In the common perception, interviewing the sex worker may seem a very attractive proposition. The tempting rustle of soft flesh ready to break into orgasmic delight at the sight of a coin, in snug boudoirs sheltered from the sins of the everyday world; copious hard-luck stories, dripping with syrup, flowing like a torrential downpour, ready to be canned for Cannes or parcelled for a Pulitzer nomination, stories of exploitation, revenge and the final emancipation from a world gone wrong.

While all this may be true in parts, in its entirety nothing could be more off the mark.

The sex worker is a tough nut to crack. Years of exploitation have calloused her soul. She will enter her cocoon and tell you to get on with the job. It's almost impossible to get her to talk. You have to wine her, dine her, cater to her every whim and become her friend before she lets you in on the dark secrets of her bizarre world. She will tell you a pack of lies in the beginning. Even her real name will not be revealed. Why should she? She is here to escape the trauma of her circumstances and not to revel in them. And you are there as a paying customer who has come to use her. Why would you want to talk, and why would she want to tell you anything?

There is also the hierarchy in the business of trafficking in women to contend with. The custodians of the sex worker, be it the pimp, the police or the politician, or anyone else, will also wonder aloud. They have money, muscle and the right connections. Prostitution is a business running into thousands of crores of rupees annually. It provides employment and very important people are fattened by it. They can get very dangerous if they sense that something doesn't fit. Why would someone visit a sex worker and part with cash only to talk endlessly? And what is he asking, and what is she saying?

Word gets around. The girls like to gossip. Brothel walls have eyes and ears and any indiscreet question can slip out, roll around like a penny and drop into the wrong hands. It takes a lot to finally extract a true story. Sometimes, you may never even get close to it.

The sex workers are great storytellers. There is great drama in their lives that seeps into their subconscious and revitalizes their imagination. It makes them happy; it keeps them alive. It is like a movie script that they like. In this case they have written the happy ending. They repeat it so many times that they start believing in it. So they will tell you stories that sound good to their ears. I have spent years listening to their gift-wrapped tales and finally, one day, they just laugh and tell me that it was all bullshit and nothing like that ever happened. They love it. It is great fun. They also love the look on your face as you realize you have been sold a dummy several times over. It's huge entertainment.

The sex worker is closely stitched to the Indian cultural ethos from ancient times. Even today, in the smaller towns and cities of India, the intermingling of sexes is not overtly encouraged. A strong pretext has to be created for it. Marriage is normally the best way to enjoy love-making without society and the law handcuffing you. But a good chunk of men who marry have already visited the sex worker and, strangely, going to a sex worker after marriage is commonplace. Most of the men I have met in brothels were married. If you are sexually deviant or your proclivities not accepted as normal behaviour, like being homosexual, for example, even your shadow may abandon you. It risks an association with what is perceived as unacceptable behaviour.

The complexities are enormous in a mammoth cross-cultural mix like India. With increased migration to urban centres, the collapse of joint families, and the legions of men with more money than ever before in their pockets floating around without their 'arranged' partners in tow, the sex industry has seen a windfall in recent times.

In the stifling social structure, it is difficult for men and women to meet even as friends. Barring the bigger cities, where women work in large numbers, in the smaller towns even frequent meetings with a male acquaintance over a cup of tea may ruin a woman's life. She will be branded a tart, and getting her married, if she is still single, will be difficult. If she is already married, she is in for more trouble. Every encounter takes place in the corridors of secrecy.

The megalopolises, though teeming with people, are paradoxically lonely places. They have a distinct contempt for the casual and meaningless conversationalist. Time is at a premium, it is money, and one is always running short of it. Intimacy is metered and doled out for advantage. Its complexion is also coated by the complications of a psyche in flux. The body and mind are adjusting to new urban spaces, and new support systems are hurriedly needed to replace the warmth of simple rural or small-town existence. The sex worker plays a huge role here. You can make her a weekend friend, and if you are keen on taking it further you can do that too. She is also alone in a way, she is also away from home, and understands loneliness and loss in an even more profound way. If she senses your quest for deeper bonding, she will meet you more than halfway. She profits from it, too.

Having been on the beat for a long time, I am often asked about the first HIV/AIDS case I covered. It was in the mid 1980s. I was working with a local newspaper and, one day, almost as soon as I entered office, I received a call from a source. 'Come immediately,' he shouted. 'Get your camera person too and shoot the first AIDS case.' He was excited. I was, too. AIDS made very big news those days. It was a scoop. So the photographer and I jumped into a cab and arrived on time at the arranged spot.

We sat in the cab, parked in the thicket of traffic, and photographed a tall, frail, thinly bearded man entering a building. After the cameraman left to develop the roll, I entered the building, met my contact and shook hands with the 'victim'. A German, he had been brought from Goa, and was being taken home to Berlin. He was accompanied by a priest. I was told that he was in the final stages of AIDS and would die soon. I was also told that he had lost about 80 kilograms. He had been a bisexual drug addict most of his life.

He was about forty-five-years-old then. In his prime he would have been a giant of a man but now he could barely walk, talk or even stand straight without holding on to something. He kept coughing. The effort ruined him. He was drenched in sweat and was breathing heavily. His shirt buttons were open and there were purple blotches on the thin skin covering his ribs.

I didn't know what to say or do. We sat looking at each other in silence. Finally, I mumbled 'God Bless' or something akin to that, shook hands (I was so scared that I went out and washed my hands at the nearest available tap), and left numbed by the meeting. The priest kept looking at all of us. He also had nothing to say. The vacuous silence was unbearable.

AIDS was scary. He looked like a weed drying out in the summer sun. I returned to office, filed a short story (the picture did all the talking without revealing the person's identity), and spent the week in contemplative silence. As a young man, it was adrenaline-pounding to cover a dangerous beat. But when you are frontally assaulted by its grotesque expression, it was terrifying. I didn't want it to happen to me or to anyone else I knew. But disease is a great leveller and I was humbled. When the time comes, the scythe would spare no one. Over the years, it reduced several people I knew to thin threads of decaying bone.

I am also asked, sometimes with sniggers, if I have slept with the women I have interviewed. It is not an innocuous question. It is loaded. Your critics assume you have chosen the beat precisely for the purpose, and even girlfriends ask you quietly in the golden moments of silence if you have strayed. 'You say you have interviewed thousands of sex workers and you also say they are gorgeous. Come on, you must have slept with some of them.' That's the everyday reasoning.

But how could I explain to anyone that I was on a dangerous beat, that I was covering the HIV, that it was a serious job. If you are covering a war, you don't go on a shooting spree! I had to be particularly careful on this beat if I wanted to stay alive to write about it.

There are also the emotional issues to contend with. Any tenderness or concern can be misconstrued for love. It happened with Rosy in one of Mumbai's 'Welcome' brothels. She got used to the endless chats, occasional gifts, outings and the pure joy of sharing without motive. One evening, after a few beers and biryani in the comfort of her spacious corner in the brothel, she jumped out of the bed with some alacrity and said, 'Give me a baby,' as though she had won the lottery. When it was explained that it wasn't such a good idea, she flared up, pulled out a key from under the pillow and opened her cupboard. It was stacked with currency notes. 'Here, take this. There is enough money for a baby. I have been working hard all these years.'

When her entreaties didn't evoke a happy response, she pulled out a blade and slashed her left wrist. The veins snapped and she lay bleeding to death on a maroon bedspread. The blood spilled out, stained the sheet a bit and dripped smoothly to the floor. The tiny blue curtain on the window looking out at the world, with ornate yellow flowers embossed on it, fluttered incongruously.

It was a frighteningly phantasmagoric sight. The adjoining rooms were packed with the calisthenics of longing, the television blared in the lounge outside, somewhere a radio jockey was asking a Bollywood actress about her current boyfriend, and customers kept trooping in. A few feet away, traffic and garbage widened the swollen roads centimetre by centimetre. Nothing made sense and yet something had to be done immediately. The madam was called, a doctor ushered and Rosy was saved amidst great drama.

Colleagues of mine have married sex workers and transvestites. Whenever we meet up, they tell me that it has been a good move. They have been happily married. Differing nationalities and cultural contexts haven't eaten into the reasons that brought them together. I have also visited the women's homes during my travels and seen the happiness that has entered their lives in the changed surroundings. A few have also become excellent biological and surrogate mothers. Not one of them has died of AIDS.

I have had many interesting, sometimes hilarious, encounters over the years. Once, while investigating Bangladeshi influx into Kolkata, I sniffed out a procurer in the market and followed him like a terrier. He took me to a godforsaken and dilapidated building and introduced me to two of the worst looking women I had ever seen. When I tried to make an excuse to slip away, he put a knife to my throat and demanded that I relieve myself of all my possessions. Faced with certain death, I made a dash towards the door Hindi-film style, sending the man and his women tumbling to the floor. I then had to jump from the second floor of the building to escape the reinforcements, and had to knock another man silly before bursting through the main gate and landing under the wheel of a two-wheeler that stopped in the nick of time!

My escapades are long and in abundance....Fasten your seat belts!

CHAPTER 1

KAMATHIPURA

Vocations which we wanted to pursue, but didn't, bleed, like colours, on the whole of our existence.

—Honore de Balzac

The heart of the flesh bazaar in Mumbai is large. But it ticks well and with efficiency. Spreading from Mumbai Central to Grant Road in the centre of the city, the flesh district is an area of frenetic commercial activity and is well connected to the suburbs by public transport, especially by railway lines.

The flesh district has roads that can torture sanity. Buses, lorries, cars, people, shops and residences cram every crevice. Not an inch of space is wasted. The decibel levels are deafening and the air is thick with pollutants. Navigating the distance can take a huge toll on one's patience. It is also one of the more rundown parts of the city, and that is saying a lot. Any sort of planning halted here ages ago. The roads need urgent repair, the craters are so huge that little children could get lost in them along with their school bags, mounds of garbage are piled up every hundred yards, several residences are propped up by wooden poles which, somehow, manage to hold up ceilings that are quite uncertain where they want to stay, and ramshackle offices add to the miasma of gloom, dilapidation and decay.

The clogged roads sneak evilly through all this. From tiny rooms and cheap, painted women on the street to the more expensive 'Welcome' brothels, from opium lairs and opulent dance-and-beer parlours to the claustrophobia of dingy hijra dens, from scores of dispensaries specializing in quick fixes for sexually transmitted diseases to ancient Chinese dentists forever promising a happy smile, from chandeliered mujra homes to pawnbrokers, jewellers, seedy lodges, grand eating houses and residences of the moral middle class still pretending to be unperturbed by the lasciviousness all around – the roads sneak through it all without query.

It's all dark and dreary. The weight of a million tragic years hangs on everything the eye can take in. But Mumbai is a city of business, of 'dhandha'. It probably understands money like no other city in the world. As long as money can be made, the status quo will remain. No one interferes in the other's affairs. All existence is delicately bonded and even a weak link in the chain is supported if there is monetary gain. It is this quest for a livelihood that passes off as the great spirit of the city. No one will complain till a calamity happens and thousands of lives are lost. Then a few fingers will be raised and a few more questions asked. By then a new cricket tournament will begin or another Hindi film released or some other catastrophe or political scam will hit another dissipating part of India (which is most likely), and all will be forgotten. Life will continue as well as it can in the confines of its limitations.

The shadows here are long and large and dark. They can hide a lot. And they hide the flesh of thousands of mothers and their young daughters ready to be picked up by soiled currency notes.

The sale of flesh takes place all over Mumbai, in the least expected areas too. The new flesh districts can take your breath away with the brazenness of their marketing and the style and chutzpah of the girls. But it's the legendary cages of Kamathipura that have given the locality a dubious claim to posterity. It is the rusty nail in the heart of the city's flesh trade. The British, it is said, used the area as a comfort zone for their troops when they were stationed here many decades ago. It is also believed that the old boudoirs were exotic and that the comfort women had international pedigree. After the British left, Kamathis, or workers from Andhra Pradesh, settled in to make cane furniture. A new generation of indigenous sex workers moved in too as the area was already well-known for its offerings. The desi (local) flavour took over completely, and Kamathipura came to be known internationally as the infamous red-light area of Mumbai.

The notorious cages that have gathered worldwide infamy are tiny rooms, measuring ten feet by ten feet or thereabouts. Concrete steps over a running gutter lead to the doorway that is barricaded by a thin, cheap and colourful nylon curtain. A wooden bed is placed in a corner of the room. Sometimes, another one is squeezed in if there is space. The girls sit outside on the steps or hang out coquettishly, all painted and dressed for the occasion. They clap loudly and call out to passers-by. If you are careless and curious and peek in, they could easily pounce on you, pull you in and rob you of your belongings. This happens all the time and so the wiser customers position themselves across the road to watch the girls rather than risk a close encounter. Once they decide whom to pick, they move in.

Blouses and skirts are short and tight. Every wrinkle, scar and asset spills out without embarrassment. Some of the girls wear trinkets and silver anklets. They are the glitz in their depressing environs, the light bulbs that fuse the darkness from casting its morbid net. Most of the girls are still leaving their teens behind and can't help being childish when no one is watching. They want to giggle and play with dolls with green eyes that close when they lie down, and they want to have eyelashes like their favourite actresses. The dolls can be named, bathed and given new clothes too. It is always nice to play mummy, and with dolls it is so easy. They are also available for a few rupees at the store just across the road.

But, for now, they have a job to do in the cages, a job that has stolen their youth even before its full flowering. If they work hard, like any schoolteacher would have told them if they ever had a chance to study, they would do well. An overdose of sex is never a great temptation after the first questions raised by galloping hormones have been well answered. But this is not a sex education class or a disco romp when you can let your skirt fall after a few drinks. This is deadly. This is life. Often, it is also death. They will play with the demon the rest of their lives.

The girls have been brought from outlying villages and sold to the brothel-keeper to sleep with men for a livelihood. They are cheap, the cheapest in Kamathipura. Everything in the vicinity is more expensive; even a decent meal costs more. The girls don't count. They don't even matter to their families, least of all to a society that replenishes and garnishes its unsteady moralistic stance by making gargantuan judgements on them. They are employed; they are sex workers. They work for a livelihood and not beg on the streets like millions of others in India. They can do without the potshots. Even the statistician employed by the government won't notice if they live or die.

A quickie can cost just a few hundred rupees. Throw in a few drinks and a heavy meal, and it's still a bargain. Little boys hang outside to run errands. There are a variety of fixes on hire. The street outside is sheer cacophony. Women, children, their pets, even parrots in cages, vendors, religious rituals, pimps, customers and a mass of human traffic shred any semblance of calm. In the tiny cages, the urgency of lust and the need to live, both auspicious reasons for the survival of Kamathipura, are separated from all the pandemonium by a torn and bleeding saree hung around the wooden bed, metaphorically barricading it from prying eyes and sounds.

The dangling saree adds to the intimacy. It demarcates the space for longing, maps the boundaries, and manages to coax the couple to remain in the territory it has secured for them. Even a toe that slips out will be seen by the world passing by, and then it will become an ugly toe ready to be gossiped about. It is much better if it is not seen. The saree, as security guard, has warmed thousands of lovers. It tells each one of them that the moment is special. There has to be a good reason to be here, to search out the dumps, to live and fornicate in them. It somehow understands that and reassures the togetherness that is taking place inside the hole. The faded cloth, slowly tearing into shreds with age, its colours running in different directions, gently holds that moment in its care, folding the orgasm in several yards. It has to keep in its possession those fleeting moments, the emotions and the spirit, that goads the bodies into desperate longing, like the darkness watching over a robbery, or the lovers may never return.

There are hundreds of girls in the cages and thousands in the area. At one level, it is a great tragedy. They have lost their childhood. Instead of studying, hanging out with friends and dreaming the fanciful infatuations that accompany growing up so endearingly, they have to make a living selling their young bodies. No man can be refused, however drunk, dirty, ugly, ill-mannered, crude or diseased he may be. All they get in return is some food, a little drink, shelter that is quite basic, pocket money to indulge in occasional shopping sprees, a toilet with water to wash up, and the camaraderie of other girls in the same predicament. There is a lot of sex, certainly much more than other girls their age in the world outside. But they can do without it. The desire here is not for sex, not at all, but for food, and don't we all know that there is no free meal in this material world. They could fall in love too, and that happens. Remember, Mumbai is a city of miracles. Sometimes, they even marry a client, and whole new vistas open up.

Lots of men live alone in Mumbai and don't have the social skills to meet the opposite gender. Or they simply don't belong to sections of society that encourage intercourse of any kind. They could be watchmen, peons, office hands, labourers, drivers or any one of the thousands of men who stream in everyday looking for jobs. It is a lonely city. They visit the red-light area, and some fall in love. It is an emotion that saves both, the men and the women, from greater desperation. If they fall into the black hole now, they will fall together. But, for most girls, especially the ones omitted from the circuit of love, it is a life of unending tragedy. Young flesh replaces the older ones soon, and then what? Uneducated and unskilled as these women are, the future holds no promise. Many of them succumb to sexually transmitted diseases, most become beggars, and some continue as sex workers and ayahs in the brothels they have worked in well into their twilight years. The luckier ones die before the frost begins to turn its screws on them.

Look at the flip side, and their new circumstances may appear kind. The girls come from the rural tracts of India. Their homes in the villages are decrepit. Food, water and shelter are seasonal. There is no electricity and no entertainment. Famines, epidemics and natural calamities ravage the land. There is no water to drink, no jobs to be had and the debt to the local moneylender increases with every arid season. Several commit suicide. There is no exit. The poverty is crushing. They have to escape the predator.

The only way out for a girl child is to get married to someone at the earliest. Child marriages still exist, and if you are not married as a child a groom is found as soon as you menstruate. If the girl's parents are poorer than the others or she is not good-looking or is unwell or even dark-skinned, this simple chore of matrimony can get very difficult. If she is physically challenged, her situation couldn't be worse. The groom, who may be sick and unemployed, is paid in cash and kind at the risk of the family being swallowed in greater debt. Very soon, she is a mother and, possibly, ill-treated after being used. She may have more children in a rush or may well become the second or third wife of an alcoholic and brutal husband. There is no source of income and no empowerment of any kind.

Her husband, the man she has been betrothed to for whatever reason, is her breadwinner. He will decide what and how much she will eat or what she will wear or who she will choose for fellowship. With him around, life is constricting. But she still has social approval, it's the done thing, and so she will accept him with all his flaws. Without him, if he dies or divorces her, life is unbearable. There will be no money for food, the children will have to be taken care of alone, and, worse, she loses face in society: she is a woman without a man now, a woman without her 'mard'. No man will want her legitimately. Another marriage is tough in these circumstances, and a relationship with a man outside the law is nothing less than blasphemy. It is scandalous and she can be killed for her indiscretion. It is an existence that stares at a blank wall.

In the brothels, at least, she gets a life. It is a difficult situation. What does she do? Both sets of circumstances are a living death.

Most campaigns to rescue women from prostitution have failed for obvious reasons. I have accompanied several such rescue teams. The girls go into hiding, and beg and plead to be left alone. The cops, social workers, politicians and bureaucrats who are part of the rescue operations, more out of the publicity they garner than any belief in the rescue, have to use force. Later, after all the hoopla of a carnival-like rescue has died down – and if they have been 'saved' and 'sent' back home – the women return to the brothels!

This is so because on returning to their villages, the girls realize that they simply don't belong to the numbing hopelessness and poverty they have left behind. They have seen too much, and too much has been done to them. The umbilical cord has been completely severed. I have met women in rehabilitation centres and also interviewed them on their return. The decision to belong to the new way of life, to prostitution and its uncertainties, is unanimous. It is a tough decision. But they have made it. Breaking in is traumatic for sure. But breaking out is worse.

Several years ago, scores of women were picked up from the brothels of Mumbai in a shower of publicity and sent home to Tamil Nadu, in a train symbolically called Mukti (Freedom) Express. Most of them had tested positive for HIV. I managed to track them to a rehabilitation centre on the outskirts of Chennai, as distant from the heart of the city as it could get. They had nothing to do, were bored, and even complained tongue-in-cheek of missing their regular quota of sex. Finally, unnoticed, they took the train back to the dingy brothels of Mumbai. Ironically, in the misery of street prostitution, they had found a reason to live. 'Life has no meaning the moment you lose the illusion of being eternal,' said Jean-Paul Sartre. For these women, slowly dying of AIDS, the brothels of Mumbai gave them the illusion of hope and kept them alive.

But there is much more to Kamathipura than the cages. The cages made news because the rest of the world couldn't believe that prostitution could fall to such depths, and so came to see it for themselves. When the word travels around the globe it gets strengthened by exaggeration. So its authenticity had to be verified.

There are the 'Welcome' brothels close by and they are a relief in comparison. They are more expensive, have a better class of women on offer, and the rooms are clean and large. The girls are also available for longer periods and can be taken by customers on their outstation jaunts for days, weeks, even for months, depending on how much is paid and the trust levels developed with the brothel madam. Normally, customers seeking companionship for an hour or more, just walk in. Every hour is happy hour. The parlours are spacious with wallpaper, sofa sets, a television sometimes, large ceiling fans and even the occasional puppy, normally a squealing pomeranian. There will be other customers waiting too, deciding on which girl to pick. Those who haven't been taken, hang around, preening themselves. If one of the girls has had a baby or is carrying, there is pure delight. They are all in line to play mummy.

The girls are dressed in line with the latest fashions, they listen to music, on ipods and walkmans now, and have mobile phones. The customer makes his choice and is taken to one of the rooms and the payment made depending on how long he wants to stay. Condoms are mandatory these days, and warm water, soap and a clean towel are issued as postcoital ritual. The 'Welcome' brothels are upmarket. They draw a highly pedigreed and loyal clientele in addition to the floater. On weekends, it is almost impossible to get a girl or a room. There is privacy, security, food, drink, lust and, sometimes, some love too for as long as one desires. An entire night could dent the pocket by a few thousand rupees.

Nearby, in adjoining lanes, are the crumbling and noisy buildings that house mujrewalis or the nautch girls. They are seated on the floor in large, carpeted rooms. Dressed in traditional Indian attire, they dance to the accompaniment of tablas and ghunghroos. They are exquisitely featured, some are breathtakingly beautiful, and hail from old schools of Indian music and dance. Without royal patronage today, they have also slipped into the underbelly. They cost a lot and choose their customers. Several are reported to be the mistresses of power brokers of the city. It is also rumoured that they have had their benefactors' progeny, and the families are kept in comfortable soundproofed walls padded with currency.

A little distance from Kamathipura, but still very much in the vicinity, the sale of flesh continues uninterrupted in Jamuna Mansion and Dreamland opposite it. Jamuna Mansion has several floors bursting at every creaking step with women from south India. They are dark-skinned, bosomy and perhaps pay more attention to personal hygiene and the cleanliness of the space they occupy. They are certainly, by all accounts, a bit too loud when it comes to personal expression. They rise individually to be heard above the collective crescendo, and that's a lot of noise. But they are a big draw. Again, for very little money, in plain speech, Jamuna Mansion remains a buyer's market.

There are hundreds of girls in the building and every small room has about ten of them spilling out. Wooden cots with plastic sheets on them are squeezed in and most of the girls sit outside in blouse and petticoat. Sarees and undergarments are done away with. It takes time to remove them, and there is no time to waste. Two couples can be squeezed in simultaneously. The others wait outside with customers, ready to move in with their partners when a bed is available. Those who haven't made any headway, display their assets a wee bit more and raise the sales pitch. Somehow, they have to make some money before the night is out. It is all fast, furious and inexpensive. Toilets are for common use, a bidet in a corner meets basic needs, and close by a stove cooks a meal. It is the most accomplished utilization of space ever. Surprisingly, the rooms are also very clean.

A few hundred yards away is Dreamland, a series of buildings with a similar theme. Countless women in little rooms are on call. There is more privacy here, a larger selection of women and higher rates. Both places are packed with customers. Ladies bars, street brothels and freelance sex workers dot the area. For some inexplicable reason, the state government has now clamped down on ladies bars. Their argument – it is corrupting the youth – is more fragile and less useful than the torn sarees that hang outside the cages. For just outside these bars, and all over the city, street prostitution is widespread.

Tara is short, less than five feet, and petite. She is in an orange saree and blouse that wraps her like an Egyptian mummy. An orange bindi, orange bangles and flowing black curly hair complete the image of a fluorescent dervish. Tara always manages a lazy drawl even when she is in a hurry; she drags her feet when she walks, her chappals scrape the ground collecting the dust with them. It is an uncommon walking style. You can't miss it; you can even hear it. Her hands are wildly flayed and her posterior rolls in exaggeration. Her gait is expansive and requires a lot of space to accommodate it. There are flowers in her thick black hair. She has sparkling eyes and a large mouth that often finds the time to smile. She keeps giggling and gesticulating; it's her way. When she is in the vicinity, it gathers you in its turbulence.

Tara was married but her husband died of an undiagnosed illness years ago. He just collapsed suddenly while ploughing the field. She looks after two young children back home in her village in Andhra Pradesh from her earnings as a sex worker in Kamathipura. Her father was a farmer and her mother, frail and blind, is still alive. Tara looks after her too. There are siblings but they have been separated from one another by the tides of time and circumstance. Tara has memories of childhood but they don't flow as easily as her laughter. She doesn't know where the others are and doesn't want to talk about the details of growing up, hungry and homeless most of the time, under the scorching southern sun. Maybe, she just doesn't want to remember the pain.

Tara was gangraped several times, had repeated abortions and several venereal diseases long before she turned eighteen, and finally found deliverance in a brothel she was sold to by her own family with the help of an agent. It is the destiny of many girls in her village. Middlemen habitually make the rounds. They know about the poverty that will always refuse to cuddle the girl child and the desperation of those tilling the land made barren by the heat and dust, repeated monsoon failures and overcropping. There are scars on her body, knife wounds and burn marks, but Tara refuses to stop smiling and offers me tea. 'If you stay longer, I will cook for you,' she says happily, 'that's if you feel like eating with me.'

Her cubicle is tiny, neatly kept, and lit by a tube light. An old ceiling fan, a trifle unsteady, whirs silently. There is a large cupboard in which she stocks up on cash, jewellery and some clothes: sarees, salwar kameezes and undergarments. She has a bank account with a nationalized bank and a passbook she is proud to show. She has 18,000 rupees in it. There is a chair, a small table with powder, lipstick and some make-up, a mirror, and pails of water under the cot. A thin brown rope stretches from one end of the room to the other with her clothes hanging on it.

The room is small, clean, cool and intimate. It gives off a good feeling, probably reflecting the aura of the occupant. There are shadows lounging around and geckos are mating on the wall. They grab one another with little gurgles of ecstasy. Tara pours me tea in small stainless steel tumblers and we sit on her large bed and talk. The bedsheet is brown and clean and the pillowcase an ugly green. Her eyes shine like expensive diamonds, maybe that's why her parents called her 'tara' or star, and she smiles all the time. I am speechless. I want to know what makes her so happy. I want to know why she is filled with so much love and how she can keep giving without being held back by the sorrow that could have turned into crust in her soul.

She lifts her saree and shows me her arms and legs. I can see knife- and burn-marks. She tells me that even her vagina has been cut up. One nipple has also been sliced off. She says all this in a matter-of-fact voice, as though reading out a child's report card. There's no drama, no tears, no look-at-my-sorry-state cry. 'How's the tea?' she then asks, smiling, trying to cheer me up. Tara is in her mid-thirties and wants to live in the brothel till the last ebb of life. 'I can't go anywhere now. This is my home. I go to my village whenever I want, I send money every month for my children's education and hope they will do well in life. There is nothing else in my life. I am a prostitute. It is my job, the lowest job ever. I am like a garbage can. Born to be used. Anyway, forget all this, tell me about you, why are you here, are you married, do you have children, how does your wife look, must be beautiful, what are your children's names, where are they studying?'

Tara charges about 300 rupees for a session, of which a portion is handed to the madam. It is a few times that for the whole night. Sometimes, she is booked for the weekends too. She keeps the tips and the gifts she gets. 'I have customers I have known for years. I have loved too but now I don't love like that, I think I have grown up. That mad, desperate love is over, thank God. My mind doesn't connect to the body. It's just a job. Many customers just want to talk and tell me their problems. They pay me because I listen. No one listens to anyone in the big city. No one has time. Everyone has problems. When I hear them, I feel my problems are nothing. I am sure even you have problems. It is the human condition. We are all supposed to have problems and we are meant to solve them. It is karma. Then we will leave this body and take another form. And, maybe, take on some new problems.'

I ask her how she knows all this. 'Is there any other reason? Look at my life. Is there any reason for all that has happened?

What have I done? I haven't even had the chance to be a bad person. I was raped as a child. So there must be something I did in a previous life and this is my punishment. When I die my punishment will be over. My next life will be good. I have done nothing wrong in this life. We have talked about this in the brothel. All the girls agree. There is no other explanation. You tell me. You are educated. If not for karma, why have we suffered like this? It is destiny, nothing else.' I look for answers. The happy geckos are also not on the wall.

I ask her about God, religion, her spirituality. Her room has several pictures of deities. Yes, she prays every day. All the girls pray. They have grown up praying to some God and the madam also insists that they pray together. 'I am born a Hindu and I pray to all the gods and goddesses. I also celebrate all the festivals. Religion doesn't matter to me. I don't know too much about all this. I haven't studied much, but there has to be some power that makes all of us so different. Even the girls in the brothel are so different from one another. How? Isn't that surprising? I feel happy when I pray. So I pray. I don't know anything else. Maybe, there is no God. I don't know. Maybe, He is not kind, maybe He is not just. I don't know all this. I just pray to what I feel is responsible for creating life. Prayer makes me feel strong and secure and happy.'

We have more tea. It is early morning. The rooms are full. Business is good like it always is. The cubicle's door is shut and there is no noise intruding into our space. A long triangular stretch of light seeps in from under the door. Some girls who have not been taken for the night sleep in the hall outside on charpoys. 'Why don't you eat? It is not good to have so much tea. There is some rice and dal. I will heat it. Let's eat,' she insists. We eat together in clean, separate plates. She gives me a spoon so that I don't dirty my hands. Tara keeps talking and giggling like a schoolgirl. She is kind and loving and wants to pamper me. 'This grain of rice has your name on it. So it is your karma to eat with me today.

Eat as much as you can. Who knows what tomorrow will bring?
We haven't seen it.'

Do you miss your kids? 'I am a mother. Which mother won't? I
am here for them. I want to live and work till they are settled. Both
are boys. So I am not worried. If they were girls anything could
happen to them. When I meet my mother I wonder what dreams
she had for me? She must have had some dreams at least. Having
become a mother, I understand my mother better.'

She has pictures of the kids framed on the wall. Two little boys,
short, thin, tanned, with oiled hair, in matching shirts and grinning
away astride a red motorcycle. It is a studio shot taken in her village.
Tara can read and write Telugu and watches a lot of television.
She loves Hindi films and sees at least one a day. Sometimes, the
girls go to the cinema close by. She likes action and romance and
even the scary flicks. 'I even saw Sunjay Dutt shooting,' she says,
all excited. 'He had come to Kamathipura.'

What's her daily routine? She normally wakes up late, but it
depends on customer traffic. If the traffic is heavy, the brothel
gets a life only at noon. Every girl gets about five customers a day
on an average. There are love stories and special customers, and
weekend and festival rush. So the numbers vary depending on
several factors. Customers can walk in anytime, some even come
to the brothel for breakfast. Some stay in the brothel for weeks
on end. Customers can stay as long as they want if they pay. But
the evenings and nights are always busy.

The madam, a former sex worker in the same brothel, wakes up
early every day and looks into the provisions and other details. The
girls who had an early night, help her. Everyone does something
or the other; duties are assigned. Some cook, other clean up, and
food is also ordered from hotels nearby. Customers may want
to drink and smoke too. Biryani, tandoor dishes and kebabs can
be ordered. On festive occasions the girls cook the dishes they

are most fond of. They don't entertain customers during their menstrual cycle but hang around and chat. It's holiday time then. They also eat out with customers. Vendors come to the brothel with fruits, vegetables, flowers, clothes, utensils, jewellery, with almost everything the girls and the brothel need. So there is no need to go out and shop unless they want to.

The brothel is spick and span. There are maids to clean up; normally they are retired sex workers. The two toilets and two bathing areas are kept spotlessly clean and disinfected, water collected in large cauldrons, floors swabbed several times a day. Condoms are used always and great stress laid on postcoital hygiene. The girls and their customers clean themselves thoroughly with water, lemon and soap. Some of them even clean up with their own urine. Lemon slices are used as a natural disinfectant. It is used for everything: washing, cooking and eating. A doctor on the street below is always available. He lives above the clinic. Sometimes the girls fall sick, but Tara has never been unwell. 'I have never fallen sick, never even had fever, I don't know why. I am so lucky. Maybe, it's my prayers.'

There is order and the brothel runs without major disagreements. Fights between the girls, though not uncommon, never last. There are some twenty girls in the brothel and Tara is one of the senior ones. The others listen to her without protest. Tara helps them come to terms with their circumstances. The girls fight over new clothes and lovers, but it's not serious. What's a little bit of ego-bruising when they have been pulverized by life?

Tara jokes and laughs till tears trickle down her eyes. I simply can't fathom her and the others in the brothel. I need constant yoga practice to still my mind and find fleeting happiness. How do Tara and the others keep laughing at life when it has always mocked them?

The Buddha talked about clinging and non-clinging. If something good happens, you have a reflexive tendency to try to hold on to it, and if something bad happens, you have a tendency to push it away. This clinging response is inevitable if you believe yourself to be the 'owner' of all the desires and fears that arise in you. You become trapped in an endless web of tension and greed.

'He who understands clinging and non-clinging understands all the dharma,' said the Buddha. This is the dharma of happiness. The alternative to the tyranny of clinging is to fully receive the experiences that arise in your life, knowing them to be pleasant when they are pleasant and unpleasant when they are unpleasant. This is the essence of living the inner life: you are enveloped by a strong sense of inner peace and spontaneity. It's quite a paradox. Life dances and you have to dance with it. Each moment is a fresh moment in the dance, and you have to be present for it.

Tara and the girls instinctively radiate the wisdom of the Buddha. Life is dancing, and Tara is dancing with it. It's the last tango in Kamathipura. It's her last dance of life.

It is late at night and traffic isn't screeching to a halt. Kamathipura has a tempo that rivals the busiest back alleys anywhere in the world. Rama Rao, a 'fence', has brought me to a building on First Lane. The rickety construction, housing over a hundred people on several floors, is kept alive by sheer willpower. One day, when it feels defeated and can't hold out much longer, it will pull the plug. Until then, it is the abode of hijras. It takes time to adjust to the darkness, to take in the putrescence of damp clothes, soiled bodies, raddled, diseased visages. If first impressions are leads, this world of sexual aberration, of eunuchs, is as revolting as it is pathetic. It is a twilight zone that is forever seeking the sun.

Rama Rao has lived in the thicket of the underbelly for over sixty years, ever since he can remember. 'I was abandoned as a baby,' he tells me. 'The hijras looked after me and brought me up. They are my "mai baap" (parents). I know everything that is happening here, and everything happens. Ask me what you want to see and I will show it.'

Rama Rao looks wise and old. His hair and beard are hennaed. Red matted locks jump out of his dark skin in agitation. His eyes are clouded with cataract and they take time to focus, but they have seen a lot.

Rama Rao is big set. He sits in a coloured lungi on a charpoy of thick woven strings. He is bare-bodied and there is thick white hair all over his chest; when he sweats he looks like marshland. He is old but not feeble, and as I look around I can see that he belongs here; like bonsai sitting pretty in a fashionable drawing room.

He is the fixer, the middleman; the one who knows all that there is to know. He is the guardian of the secret vault, privy to the evils of the inner sanctum. His ears, grey hair sprouting out of them venomously, like cacti looking for sunlight, are kept to the ground. He has all the connections. 'Big people come to me. I know what they want, and I deliver the best "maal" (stuff).' He won't divulge names. 'You also know what I mean,' he says matter-of factly, looking me hard in the eye. 'I have seen you here many times.'

Garbage has piled up on the road outside in huge, smelly heaps. Large, well-fed flies are annoyed by the stray dogs foraging food, gaudily-painted sex workers have taken positions, the 'Welcome' brothels are overflowing with flesh and lust, and customers are barging in and out of the innumerable brothels in a frenzied shopping spree for young, tender, compliant flesh that often costs little more than a bottle of rude country liquor. You can empty entire factories of disinfectant here, and even the malarial mosquitoes won't wince.

Later, in the same building, I am in a little room. It is a musty, dingy crevice in the wall, irregularly framed as though a bomb had made a crater. I am scared and nervous. The resolute safety of the audacious cacophony outside has been barred entry by a monstrous door. Iron grills on tiny windows high up the damp walls seal my fate. In the semi-darkness are black, heaving breasts, held together somewhat but still spilling out of regulation white, cotton bras. 'I was barely seven years old when I was raped. Ever since I have only been interested in men,' says Mohan, now Sheela. 'Women revolted me.' The words seize me in a stranglehold. I know I can't escape. I am condemned to listen to her. I have asked for it. It is easy to latch on to every word. The silence in the little hole says nothing to distract me.

After a few years at school in Dindigul in Tamil Nadu in south India, Mohan took up a contractual job as an unskilled labourer in a company manufacturing heavy machinery; one of several that he found to feed his hunger. His sexual proclivity was pronounced from childhood and his escapades as a homosexual started early. He was fair game for the men. They had him several times as a young boy, and he just loved every moment. He enjoyed being brutalized, and went miles for the pain. He had a sweet, feminine face and the tanned, lithe body of an antelope on the run in the Savannah. It was all so pleasurable, and when he started getting paid for his hormonal charge, he thanked the Maker with all his heart. He knew that he would never be unemployed and, even better, would love the job.

The youngest of eight children born to landless labourers, Mohan's childhood was deficient in the basics. Two meals a day had to be scraped with difficulty. His mother died of an illness that 'stole her flesh every day', his father married again, and more children were born. Misery piled on misery. School didn't last long and he took any job he was given to survive. One day he was repeatedly raped in the fields. 'But, strangely, I loved it,' he says. 'I craved the violence of sex. The men found me beautiful and I became an expert lover. I learnt how to make a full grown man beg for more.'

As he grew older, Mohan began to exaggerate the femininity he carried within. He loved wearing a saree and dolling up. His manners, gestures, walk, the way he talked, every aspect of his being, carried the seed of muliebrity waiting to germinate into a wild flower. Then his father died mysteriously, again to some strange disease that sucked his insides out, as he puts it, and the family broke up. The siblings went their ways. His sisters, he believes, became sex workers. There was no other way.

But Dindigul is a small town forever inhabiting the safety of the past. You are easily noticed if you are different, and if you run on the margins of convention you are reported. Mohan got to be a huge embarrassment. The tight social boundaries were closing in on him. He had to be tethered. Normally, marriage is suggested as ideal suffocation. It is the panacea for unconventional behaviour. But with no family to make this happen and social norms tightening around him like a noose, Mohan got into a train for Chennai, a big city, and not too far away. He had to run away and make his hay under a more brilliant sun.

It was the first time that he had seen a big city and he enjoyed every bit of it. He worked as a freelance sex worker in the Egmore-Marina beach belt. 'I did whatever was asked of me. I did it for the money. I never said no,' says Mohan. 'I started doing well. I had grown taller and put on weight and started looking like a woman too. But I had a penis and I hated it. He had hundreds of customers. One day a man picked me up thinking I was a woman. I was soliciting at Marina beach late in the evening. I was dressed in a saree and had flowers in my hair. I had a lot of jewellery too. He took me to his room, had a few drinks, undressed me and saw my penis. He was enraged. He hit me and nearly killed me.' It was then that he decided that, somehow and very soon, he had to knock that penis off. A male organ in a saree could be a fatal nexus.

Mohan had some money now, a few contacts and many ambitions. He had met others on the beat and they unanimously recommended Mumbai as a career move. And that's exactly what he did. He had an address in Bhandup in the far-flung suburbs of the city. Mohan got off the train at Dadar TT one sunny afternoon clutching a little bag because 'in Mumbai, you can do exactly what you want and no one cares'. And then he ran untamed in the dream city.

A few months later, Mohan moved from Bhandup to Kamathipura to a brothel shared by fifteen other eunuchs. They were all from Dindigul and other neighbouring towns in Tamil Nadu. They spoke Tamil, cooked sambar and dosa and felt at home. Mumbai has several areas of eunuch prostitution but Kamathipura suited him the best. 'Lots of men come here,' Mohan tells me seriously about the business he is in. 'We fall in love too.' He is animated now. 'They come from everywhere, from the richest families and the best jobs, with beautiful wives. They come to us because we are great at love-making. That's what they tell us. Why would they come to us otherwise?'

He has a point there. His digs are horrendous. The surroundings worse: garbage piled high, open drains oozing stench, defecation and infection; semi-naked child-women and eunuchs with their hormone-enriched assets spilling out of dirty blouses and torn skirts, eczema scaling their abused bodies; pimps and hustlers in mufti and uniform; and after all this, the rainbow at the end of the grind – man-woman with extended teats, juicy thighs and handcrafted vaginas. Still they beckon the male hormone in droves – there must be a twist to that testosterone or in the holy matrimony that now entraps it in domesticity!

Their rates compare well with those of the female sex workers in the vicinity. A few hundred rupees a day is the average earning.

Since they live together and take turns cooking and cleaning, expenses are reduced. There is enough for outings and other extravagances. It is a good life, certainly better than living at home manacled to a loveless family and scratching a livelihood while being ridiculed forever for being different. They have one another too. They understand each other's emotional, physical and spiritual needs and believe that if they are 'good' now, they will be delivered from this wretchedness in the next birth.

Once a year, they go back to their villages, fattened by the pickings of their trade in Mumbai. It is a strange homecoming. They are full-blooded women now, albeit hand-embroidered. They are no longer the butts of ridicule. The village will only remain the soil where the daffodil took birth. The city is where it was nourished. The old legend too gets another lease – go to Mumbai and grab your gold!

A few years ago, Mohan got castrated at a local hospital. After the two-and-a-half-hour operation, he metamorphosed into Sheela. The pain was acute, he says, and he slept without dreams for days. But ever since, her (Sheela now) feminine contours have been rapidly filling out. She has had hormone injections and is now an Amazon with enormous assets and a smooth body. The soft padding of flesh on her buttocks and thighs accentuates her femininity.

She giggles, stretches her huge bosom, notices the impact it is having on me, and almost undresses on the pretext of showing me the marvels of modern medicine. Tube lights have been switched on, music is blaring away on the radio and she gets effusive, heaving away, one hand gently measuring my trembling thigh.

Hijras love to shock. They love the effect they have on men. It can be terrifying. You can't look away, they can't be ignored, and, normally, a mysterious fear can paralyse the recipient of their advances even if he is prepared for it. You are also curious and want to see and touch, it's all so different, but wonder how to react and what to say. Outright rejection can inflict more psychological pain. You are then treading dangerous ground, and if you want to nip the advance before it gets startling you have to do it gently, coating it with humour, so there is no perceived affront. It is a delicate act.

The castrations are normally done in hospitals and, more informally, by 'Dai Mas' or senior eunuchs, in the most unhygienic conditions. Hospitals have strict procedures. An ethical committee of three psychiatrists should certify the absence of penile erection. There are other physical and psychological parameters too and only after the examining committee is convinced that a woman is trapped in a man's body is a sex change operation allowed.

The 'Dai Ma', though, is easier to convince and far less embarrassing to approach. He is a senior eunuch and understands the distress and the need to go through the gender change at any cost. He has also lived through the experience. No questions are asked, but the operation is primitive. There is no anaesthesia; only alcohol to numb the pain. The penis and testicles are sliced off the body with a knife. Hot oil is poured on the wound. It stops the bleeding and also serves as an antiseptic. Then, to prevent the urethra from closing, a neem stick is inserted into it and oil poured into the opening with a hot rod. Post-operative care is crucial. A high protein diet is essential to recoup. The 'patient' also needs to abstain from sex for a few weeks at least for the recovery to be complete.

The castration ceremony is an elaborate procedure studded with ritual. The newcomer has to fast and pray for ten days. All prayers are to Goddess Amba. The castration is performed on the eleventh day. Those attending the ceremony stand naked. A black silk thread tied around the genitals is skilfully used. Sometimes, it can be a knife sterilized on a candle flame.

The castration ceremony is like delivering a child. On the sixth day the eunuch is given a new name. On the twenty-first day she is allowed to get up and move about. During this period she is treated with great care. After a bath in boiled water with neem leaves soaked in it to purify her, she visits the temple with other eunuchs to pray for strength, hope and fulfilment in the new life. The new hijra is welcomed with great ceremony and a 'guru' or 'mother' tutors her in the ways of the new world.

Eunuchs fall into three categories: masculine, feminine and muscular feminine.

The masculine ones are not normally castrated. They are generally well-muscled and hirsute. Feminine eunuchs are beautiful by any yardstick. They are soft and coquettish. Castration and hormone therapy chisel their femininity further and they become the femme fatales of the group. The muscular-feminine ones have characteristics of both genders.

Most eunuchs suffer from serious psychological disorders that remain with them all their lives. Sheela believed that she suffered from chronic sexual dysfunction and wasn't a complete man. She also hated women because she thought that she could never become one. But when she was treated for venereal diseases before her sex change, it was discovered that she did have a normal erection and adequate seminal discharge.

'I love being a woman,' Sheela says happily. 'I feel so complete now.' Her duties in the brothel are that of a homemaker's. She wakes up early, prepares the food for the others, washes clothes, irons them and does the cleaning. She takes a short afternoon nap and decks herself for the evening when customers either come over or she decides to go to their place.

She loves dressing up in brassy, provocative sarees, her long, black hair oiled and combed and smelling of fresh jasmine and marigolds. She adorns herself in gold, silver and trinkets, paints her toes and fingernails dark red, pencils her eyebrows, adds a large, round red bindi on her forehead, and slaps thick lipstick and several coats of talc on her face to look fair and desirable. An overstated gyration of her ample hips, shrewd, calculated 'pallu' droppings, the large, full mouth perennially red and pouting with paan (betel nut leaf), and the born-again courtesan strides into the night for a kill.

Who would have ever imagined that the young Mohan forever running from the law and from society in the dusty, hot, impoverished tracts of a nondescript village in south India – for being 'different' – would one day streak into India's glamour city thousands of miles away in the guise of male candy? Was this the gold that Mumbai offered?

All eunuchs don't end up as well-paid sex workers, though. Some survive by singing and dancing at birth and death ceremonies; others are busy with domestic chores. Many just beg on the roads and make a nuisance of themselves with their customary noises of extortion. Their curses come true, it is said, and if angered they can lift their sarees and display their genitals publicly along with a blast of choice invectives in voices that haven't decided on which gender to reside in. It can all get very unsettling.

This is what most people don't want and they readily give in to the hijras' demands. Hijras are also sometimes the bizarre pieces in the rich array of offerings at high-society parties. Dance bars also embellish their item numbers with a hijra dance. A svelte hijra joins the party and pirouettes in harem clothes amid wolf whistles from a male audience throwing currency notes.

'We are finally happy,' says Sheela. 'We have an identity now, we are not imprisoned in a body we don't want.' Her friends in the brothel, Reema and Jaya, nod their heads in agreement. But the great sorrow in their lives is that they will forever remain barren. There are several other problems of fitting into a world that they can never ever belong to. 'The police harass us all the time and extort money,' they complain in unison.

But all this is of little significance. Having finally become women, they now want to become mothers, to create a new life, and to hold close to their new bosoms their own flesh and blood. Any togetherness, until now, has been a commercial transaction. At least, as mothers, the love could be without strings.

It is also difficult to head back home after all this. They have travelled a long road. The past has been struck dead. 'I will never go home,' says Sheela. 'I have three brothers and four sisters, all married and happy. I am a "kalank" (disgrace) to the family. I can never show them my face.' She lowers her face, comes closer and whispers as though the whole world is dying to sell her secret for a million bucks, 'You know, I am married. My "mard" is waiting for me in the village.' She is hallucinating, and why not? It is a bite of the baggage that rests, unwieldy and burdensome, on her new, soft shoulders. What harm can a little make-believe do? Even if it can't prevent the plaster from falling off the ceiling, it may cushion the senses when dreams are dead. What's a little bit of rouge when the trapdoors are shut and the keys thrown into the distant oblivion of an unending twilight zone?

Hijras are known to operate in many tiers. The 'alis' are transsexuals. They are men who have chosen ritual castration. They live off the sex trade and dress and behave like women. Then there are the 'dangas' and 'panthis'. The 'dangas' have strong feminine traits that are generally under cover but which find passionate expression in the right conditions. They are receptive partners. 'Panthis' have a masculine identity and play the role of the male partners. The fourth tier is that of the 'doubledeckers'. They are not overtly feminine or masculine and play both roles: they are males with the 'dangas' and females with the 'panthis'.

There is also the annual Aligal Thiruvizha, or the eunuch festival, every April at the Koothandaver temple in Kooragam, some 40 kilometres from Puducherry. The legend behind the temple celebrations revolves around Mohini, the enchantress. According to folklore, during the battle of Kurukshetra, the Pandavas had to sacrifice a warrior to defeat the Kauravas. Aravanan was chosen for the sacrifice. As a last wish, he expressed a desire to get married. Since the women knew that whoever married him would get widowed in a day, none volunteered to be his wife. So Lord Krishna appeared in the form of Mohini and married him. Eunuchs consider Aravanan their lord and master because he married a woman who was actually a man.

Eunuchs who attend the Koothandavar festival enact the marriage ceremony on the last day of the ten-day festival by tying 'mangalsutras' on the temple priest who stands in for Lord Aravanan. The revelry continues throughout the night, which is always a full-moon night, and in the morning the idol is consigned to the flames. The eunuchs mourn the death of their husband by breaking their bangles and donning widow whites. The festival has changed these days with a beauty contest added to the festivity.

Hijras also marry among themselves. The eunuch who is the wife wears a 'mangalsutra' and dances while the husband plays the 'dholak' at the marriage ceremony. If the husband dies before she does, the wife lives like a widow. They have an eerie funeral procession too to add to the shades of twilight that they cohabit so precariously. It is carried out silently in the dead of night. The corpse is propped up, sometimes with sticks, and made to 'walk' to the pyre. There is no mourning. Instead, there is rejoicing.

An unfortunate life has ended. The cortege prays that he never takes birth as a eunuch again.

A lot has changed in Kamathipura. The odour of decay continues its deathly watch over the dilapidation but there is no space for new brothels, and police raids are pushing the women to new regions in the northern suburbs. The closure of ladies bars has also resulted in a more even spread of prostitution all over the city. There is also talk of developing Kamathipura into prime real estate. The city is choking on all sides and the authorities are looking at reinventing available real estate.

This will be good for Kamathipura. It may get roads that don't duck for cover in the monsoon, buildings that smell good with new paint, and some clean air to breathe. It may also lead to new, better, more legitimate flesh districts in the city accessed more readily by medical aid and the messages of safe sex.

It has also become difficult to interview the girls. They look at every question with suspicion. If you don't get on with the job soon and hang around a bit, they think you are an agent of the government snooping on them, and then they just clam up and ask you to leave. Several raids, intentioned to rescue them, have actually slaughtered them. They have nowhere to go.

The sex worker has already lost everything in her life. Her 'izzat' (honour) has been sliced away so many times that she doesn't even remember how and when it happened the first time.

Where will she hide? Even the night sky has eyes.

For *Fallen Angels*, a book on sex workers in South Asia, my colleagues and I might have interviewed over a thousand girls. We were visitors, and, yet, the harsh life of the flesh trade had charred us. Several colleagues fell violently sick. A producer from a British television company got bronchitis in four days and a few others fell ill with tuberculosis. Every single one of us was broken inside and we still carry the scars tattooed on us.

'For many of us who have spent much of our lives working with sex workers, these women are our gurus,' says John Frederick, editor of *Fallen Angels* and an expert on prostitution and the trafficking of women in South Asia. 'Again and again, as I sat in the brothels with the women as they told me about their lives, they would suddenly smile, reflecting on a moment of kindness in their years of hell. This netherworld of prostitution is our classroom, and the sex workers are our teachers. The conferences, publications and noble pronouncements of those who fight against trafficking and slavery are meaningless gestures unless we sit at the feet of our teachers, and acknowledge their wisdom, marvel at their resilience, and laugh with them.'

About the brothel raids that have harmed the girls immensely, Frederick believes that the raids happen because, 'Regular people are afraid of sex workers. The thought of sex disturbs them, the suspicion of their power disturbs them. Regular people are made uncomfortable by sex workers as they are made uncomfortable by the HIV-positive, by yogis, by the disabled, by saints and by the insane. Power is discomfiting and sex workers have immense power and knowledge, particularly over men.'

CHAPTER 2

LADIES BARS

Don't tell me the moon is shining; show me the glint of light on broken glass.

—Anton Chekhov

The ladies bars, which shot into the media spotlight in recent times when they were banned, are places where men spend a lot of money to watch beautiful women dance – an extravagant but harmless way to spend time. The women charge enormous amounts for more private sessions, and very few men can afford them. Those who can are only getting rid of ill-gotten wealth. Most business transactions in India involve payments under the table, and ladies bars are a good way to get rid of the money that can't be stored in banks or used through credit cards and cheque books. The parallel economy in India is colossal, and this is an excellent way of mopping up black money. The morality issues that have been raked up to support the ban don't have the desired result as the girls simply disappear and find similar employment with a different calling card.

At the bars the women dance energetically and with an imaginative show of skin to loud Hindi film music rich in innuendo and beat. They are in sarees and other traditional Indian costumes and their dances look far less obscene than the 'item' numbers that sell Hindi cinema at the box-office. Men shower the girls they fancy with currency notes that are picked up by attendants and dropped into boxes set aside for such collections. The dancers take a portion of the largesse. The management decides what to do with the rest.

Several people in positions of power have to be paid to allow all this to happen. It is widely accepted that hundreds of thousands of rupees are dropped into the boxes in the ladies bars every single night. It is quite a spectacle: non-stop dancing, strobe lights, loud music and scores of men seated around tables drinking, eating and ogling away. A hijra dance is also added to mix if the management feels like it.

At erratic intervals, a man beckons a girl with currency notes or he just walks over to the dance floor and garlands her with money. Some men join the dancers too to the accompaniment of wolf whistles and loud appreciation. Everyone has a great time. Bouncers keep a close watch and there is never any ruffle in the proceedings. The bars are all owned and run by unlikely bedfellows brought together by the lure of quick and big money, and born without a chartered accountant's whistle or a padre's conscience.

With the closure of these bars, the sex industry has another arm. Thousands of women without education have lost their livelihood. They have to cash in on their looks before the passage of time wrinkles it. So they have slipped into the flesh industry in every corner of the city, or moved to other states in India and even to different countries. Sex workers have a very short shelf life. They have to mint the moment even if the sun has temporarily blighted it.

I have interviewed several bar girls. Most of the interviews have taken place in the green room. It is a little room with mirrors and benches, painted in innocuous cream or pastel shades, with a toilet attached to it. It is very basic. There are containers of talc, soaps, make-up kits, a few combs and towels. You finish your dance, rush in, change clothes and prepare for another round. You adjust your make-up in the large mirror, ask the others how you look, take a final glance, and you are off. There is no time even for gossip.

After the show, the girls change into ordinary, everyday clothes, and finally get a chance to yak away. They will talk about the money earned and about the customers. Some of them will accompany clients for the night, but most of them will go home to families that they look after with their earnings.

It is very late at night, early morning really, when they pack up, and they don't need more attention on the way home. So make-up, jewellery and all the glamorous outfits are removed and they get into a dowdy salwar kameez if they can. Groups of women don't always travel at this time of the night and so they are a visible presence. Cabs wait outside the bars. They share them to their destinations somewhere in this lonely, dreary city or to the nearest railway station if they are living far away.

Lata is from Agra, from a 'basti' (one of several hutments) near the Taj Mahal. She says she is twenty-seven and married with two children. Her husband has left her, the children are in school, and she takes care of old and sick parents. She is slightly built and wears spectacles when she isn't dancing. Her features are soft. She isn't garrulous like the others and can pass off as a chemistry teacher at a municipal school. She has a stern look and a commanding air. You will never imagine that she makes a living dancing to currency notes.

'I make good money,' she tells me. 'But it is hard work. You know how it is. Dancing for so many hours every day is not easy.

My feet pain every night and I need to be massaged. I have varicose veins and take medicines. Every man thinks we are game. I haven't been to anyone till now. I dance, collect the money and go home. I have many responsibilities. My children are in an English-medium school and my father has "lakva" (paralysis). I have to look after them. If something happens to me, they are finished. I can't even afford to fall sick for a day. I pray to God that nothing happens.'
I ask her if she has given a thought to marriage again. 'No, I will never marry again,' she retorts fiercely. 'It is no use. I will have more kids and more problems. I am very happy without a man. Who needs a man anyway? I am earning well. I can also get sex anytime I want, so why do I need a husband? Marriage is just legal prostitution.'

Rani is also from Uttar Pradesh. She is also in her twenties and is married with children. Her husband is still with her but doesn't contribute to the household. 'He drinks all the time and doesn't work. If I don't give him money, he hits me. I don't really care about him, he can leave me and go if he wants to, but I am worried for my children. Nothing should happen to them. I should secure their future. That's my only concern.'

Both girls have bank accounts and have made small investments. They met in Mumbai and have become good friends. They dance at the same bar, live in the same building, go shopping together and help look after each other's families. They understand each other well. They also go home to their villages together, at least once a year. They don't have to tell the world what they do for a living. It's their secret. The job provides for the family and gives them the dignity that money can buy.

Shama is glamorous and very attractive. Even while talking to me, she keeps checking her make-up and looks into her little mirror. She knows she is beautiful. She has the look of a woman who enjoys the attention of men. She is also about twenty-seven and married with kids. She is from Delhi. All the three – Lata,

Rani and Shama – are from poor families. They have studied till the third or fourth standard and then dropped out. Educating girls is considered unnecessary in poor Indian families. They will anyway get married and leave home. They are 'paraya dhan' or someone else's wealth. So they are taught housework. All the three were married off in their teens and their parents rustled up large amounts of dowry. Unfortunately, all the three husbands turned out to be useless, good-for-nothing jerks. They spent the dowry and took to drinking, gambling and womanizing. The girls are the only earning members in their families and, worse, they run the risk of contracting a sexual disease from their husbands!

I meet these girls while talks are on about the impending ban on bar girls. They have read and heard about it and are obviously worried. What will you do if the bars really shut down, I ask. 'We will have to go to other cities or somewhere else in Mumbai. We don't know what to do really. But something will have to be done. Whatever is written in our "naseeb" (destiny) will happen.' They know that they can't dance forever and have to make quick money and bank it somewhere, possibly even start a small shop or enterprise. The sooner they do this the better. It all depends on how much money they have to kick-start a new venture. For now, prostitution is the only recourse and they recognize that fact. It is lucrative.

'We will have to take to "dhandha",' they tell me without sounding alarmed. They have obviously thought about it. 'What else can we do? We have no other skill.' Some girls have made contacts with bar owners in neighbouring states. Some have decided to move out of the country. The sex industry all over the world has sent feelers to the bar girls. Most of the girls are attractive and dance exceptionally well. They are checking out options. The girls and their managers meet up frequently to discuss plans. But their lives will be disrupted. Children's schooling, parents' medical treatment, new employers and clients, a new country altogether; every aspect of their lives will be turned upside down. It's a big move and they are very uncomfortable with it. But there is no choice. If they don't dance fast and furious now, the wide net of everyday, unkind prostitution will eventually suck them into its intricate folds.

India is multicultural and the sex industry underscores this well. The girls are from different faiths and communities. There are no caste, communal or religious differences. If they group together for any reason, it is only for the easy governance of the brothel. If food habits and other cultural needs are common, there will be more harmony. That's all. There is no time or reason for religious quarrels. They come from all parts of India. The trade has a strong Nepali presence too. Thousands of girls are trafficked from Nepal. They look different. They are fair, well built and well dressed, and a big attraction. There is also a large representation from Bangladesh. Closeted with drugs and disease of every vintage, the sex industry melts precariously on the long wick of a slow burn.

The festive season begins in India in September and continues till March. It is a particularly profitable period for the sex workers. Men have got their annual bonuses, it is holiday time, the weather is pleasant and the mood is conducive for reckless experimentation. The flesh trade is busy throughout the year but, like all businesses, it is also subject to the seasons. The monsoon months can be bad for business. And if there are communal riots and, possibly, a curfew as a result, customers won't stir out. Repeated police raids are also a dampener. But, by and large, enough money is made for basic necessities.

The customers also have it tough. Once you go to a sex worker, it is difficult not to return. Of all the vices in the world, this is the most difficult to discard. Many men become sex addicts. The constant need for sex for either gender, according to analysts and counsellors who have worked with me and helped out with the rehabilitation processes, is a chronic psychological disorder. Many sex workers, despite the overdose, also suffer this need.

I have interviewed hundreds of customers, many of whom are sex addicts – ordinary men from regular families – boasting thousands of conquests even before turning thirty. The lifetime sexual excursions of a Hollywood hunk credited with Neanderthal biceps will be surpassed in a week by the average brothel addict. Nearly all of them are married or in steady relationships. They can socialize with a choice of women in their workplaces and they do consort with what can be called some very 'accomplished' women. Yet, for some inexplicable reason, they are hooked to the sex worker. She has a strange appeal and they can't shrug it off. It is a myth that single men visit the sex worker. The loneliness in marriage can be aggressive. The sex worker understands that and knows what to do.

CHAPTER 3

COLABA AND KALA GHODA

Times bitter flood will rise
Your beauty will perish and be lost.
                                        —W.B. Yeats

Colaba and Kala Ghoda are venerable and elegant neighbourhoods at the southern tip of Mumbai. They emerge, if one were to travel close to a straight line, from the picturesque Flora Fountain, which is within easy reach of both the train stations. Kala Ghoda has fashionable eating houses, offices from where legitimate businesses are conducted, and a sprinkling of art galleries. Most of the architecture is Victorian. It is a pedigreed locality of Mumbai. To the east of Kala Ghoda are the docks where large ships are berthed. They have come to recuperate from gruelling voyages. They will be repaired and readied to take the call of the sea head on. Walk a few minutes further south and, before the army cantonment, you enter the throat of Colaba. And then, suddenly, you are catapulted from the genteel, easygoing saunter of Kala Ghoda to the hustle and frenzy of tourists.

Colaba is a delightful area with the magnificent Taj Mahal Palace Hotel watched closely by the Arabian Sea, old houses, noisy colonies of fisher folk, and denizens who sprout from nowhere to cajole the white man to part with his dollar. The pavements are packed with bric-a-brac and hard bargains, a variety of intoxicants are on offer, and tiny rooming inns that are spread out like mosquito bites stealthily embarrass every definition of sin with the liaisons that grow in their cunning environs.

Walk on, past the smell of fish and disorder, and you enter the rarified confines of the military establishment, all spit, polish and discipline, and as removed from the street next door as can be imagined. It has large, open spaces and carefully cultivated greenery. Sparkling military vehicles pass by to ramrod stiff backs and smart salutes. The area is also heavily patrolled and foreigners need permission to stroll around. Army cantonments are sensibly kept away from the unwashed street. For the traveller and the tout, this order holds no fascination. He is not here to comb the area with a toothbrush. He is not looking for the army's confidential files. He needs the sultry smooch of oriental exotica sold to him by strident street calls.

Colaba has for long been the hideout of desperadoes. It also housed the flower children, the early hippies, and travellers of various hues. It is an attractive destination and far cheaper and more secure than other similar attractions bordering India. It is well located (Goa and Pune are a few hours away), well serviced round the clock with continuous power, water and public transport, has post offices, internet cafes, banks, hospitals, gardens, hotels, discos, eateries and brothels. The nightlife has wholesome offerings, the cuisine on offer excellent, and almost anything can be had for a few dollars. For the backpacker seriously considering a moment of luxury, the Taj is always at hand, and there is also Leopold, the cafe that wears bullet marks on its sleeve and serves large casks of beer and wholesome international cuisine. Restaurants have jukeboxes and entertainment can also be had at the Regal cinema. And when you feel like dropping out and watching the world go by against a backdrop of ocean liners and sundry merchant vessels, just stretch out on the promenade that extends from the Taj to the Radio Club a few hundred yards away. Of course, the hustling won't stop but you can tune in to the soft drone of the Arabian Sea forever splashing away.

The Colaba police station has its hands full. Quite like its counterparts in other police stations, it is forever collecting hush money. This is another reason why the area is so safe for the lawbreaker. I lived in Colaba for several years, in impersonal, dingy rooms by the sea, where the rain and the sun would walk in and leave without asking, and made friends with its weaknesses. Tiny rooms at exorbitant rates were let out for all sorts of needs. Landlords, most of them mere tenants but protected by the law with rents frozen for decades, lived quite well off the amounts that they earned from sub-letting the premises. Every year these little bed spaces cost more and inflation was effectively combated.

Some, like me, chose the area for convenience. Colaba has room service round the clock and you can escape the choke of commuting which, specially for newcomers to the city, can be a harrowing experience. Colaba also gave you a vantage position to watch life unfold as smoothly as a hungry boa constrictor setting out for food. It didn't come cheap, though; the rents left very little in your pocket but it was well worth it. The real estate agents knew that. For others, it was the headquarters of the marketplace. They could buy and sell anything, without hiding their faces, to a travelling international community that was willing to spend on experimentation.

These cubbyholes, where you couldn't squeeze in Iyengar yoga without knocking the plaster off the wall or deforming your spine, were safe places for the sale of drugs and sex. If needed, plans were also hatched from these soulless rooms to settle personal scores. For a price, the object of your dislike could be maimed or murdered. It was all too easy and well-organized. There were takers for everything. Colaba also never let out its secrets to those who minded their own business. You could share the apartment with a hardcore criminal and he would be more civil with you than your wife was during the early days of courtship. You would, of course, have to draw the line; no probing, no uneasy questions and you would have a smooth ride. There would never be midnight knocks on personal space.

I once had an apartment mate (I changed rooms over twenty times) who spent the day packaging hashish balls. He would take out long thick, black strips running into several feet, cut them up into tiny balls or 'golis' the size of marbles, count out about ten of them, place them in small plastic containers and seal them over a candle flame. He made hundreds of packets every day and sold them to touts. He made a good living. He could afford the rent. Incidentally, we lived opposite the police station and I was a reporter in a leading newspaper!

I used to peek in, opening the door ever so lightly, and watch him. He would return my gaze with a look-at-the-things-one-has-to-do-in-life grin and continue packing the hashish. But he had an ardent devotee. Tits, my name for the matronly, brown dachshund with mammary glands that scraped the floor when she waddled along, loved the hashish. Tits shared the apartment with us. She would nose the door open every morning at the appointed hour, wag her tail and smile charmingly, bite into a 'goli' and step out into the living room for a day of peace and joy. When she woke up from her hallucinations hours later (she used to lie on her back and moan and giggle), she dug into her beef mince and cod liver oil and spent the day in contentment. Tits was sixteen years old and had finally become a junkie after a lifetime of pandering to the attentions of the dogs in the locality.

In another apartment I rented, the landlady had a high-class sex worker as a tenant, a nice, young, educated, well-constructed woman who used to help me with the cooking. She would buy vegetables and chicken from the market and prepare a meal we both tucked into with relish. I would get the wine. Before pushing off for work, she would give me a cheery 'hi' and ask if she looked good enough to eat. She knew that I knew what she did, and we joked about it. I loved the gusto with which she went to work. It is rare even in the most high-profile jobs. Sometimes, she insisted that I join her on shopping sprees and late dinners. I shared digs with gangsters, their molls, winners of beauty pageants, professional killers, and even with an accountant who was contemplating suicide because he was going bald. Of all my apartment mates, he was the most difficult to handle.

You did what you wanted in Colaba. No one cared as long as you didn't tread on toes. It was as secure as IBM's solutions for tomorrow. With its colour and its accessories, Colaba remains the ideal distraction for a wide description of people.

As a journalist and inveterate street watcher, I enjoyed meeting every type. But I preferred the renegades and the odd balls. They were more fun. I guess I liked to live vicariously; there was a thrill in watching and being with people who did what I couldn't. I was too scared to break the rules but there was a grudging admiration for those who could. I was burdened by the strains of societal judgement, while they were so completely free from conformist pressures. I just marvelled at those who looked rules in the eye and told them to go for a hop.

I remember seeing a short, dark, squat middle-aged bearded man in dowdy ill-fitting shirts and slacks and in broken sandals sitting on the promenade for months on end. He did nothing but smoke, but whenever a constable on the beat passed by he received a smart salute. Intrigued, I befriended him. We hung out together for months, shared a few smokes and then he let out one day with a chuckle that he was wanted by Interpol for multiple murders in his country. He had no reason to trust me, but the point here was that he didn't care even if I let out his secret (if what he was saying was indeed true). He knew that he was safe and would remain untouched. He had run away, crossed international borders, and had taken refuge in Mumbai. He was in no danger here, he said. All he had to do was pay the cops.

He stayed for years and then disappeared as suddenly as he had arrived. One day, he wasn't there, and no one knew where he had gone. He had vanished. Just like that! I asked around. Even those who met him regularly said that they had never known such a man. In an instant, someone who had been there for, maybe, a decade, wasn't even a memory. The silence, I realized later, was essential. It made Colaba so special, and kept it alive to unending excitement. It also made a great deal of sense because India affords witnesses no protection. If you squeal, you are a goner.

It was during one of my several wanderings here that I first met Rita, in an Irani restaurant in a tiny lane off the Taj Mahal Palace Hotel. Tall, fair, slim and busty, she flashed me a smile that connected my soul to an electric house. I had walked in for a hurried bite. There was a cup of tea on her table and no companion to share it with. Would you like to join me, she gestured with her expansive eyes. I looked around, the other tables were occupied, and decided to join her. She had a tiny white top, blue hot pants, blue chappals and a black bra. The strap was visible. Her tiny eyes indicated that she could be Chinese, Tibetan, Nepali or from the northeast of India. She was a stunner, with friendly but lonely eyes. Her legs seemed to travel endlessly, like a stretch limo, from a body that would have made the sun tremble at noon or possessively cover her with a shadow.

I had left adolescence behind a few years ago with considerable ceremony but I thought she gave me a sudden crop of acne. I sat nervously beside her and ordered a cup of tea. The waiter looked at me and smiled, but the others in the restaurant didn't raise an eyebrow. I had no idea that this eminently desirable woman seated next to me was a hooker and that she did this frequently. I thought, in my naivete, that she liked me and had made a pass.

'I am Rita,' she said in easy English, without delay, and held my hand in her soft palms. My heart leapt out in loud thuds. There was a magical quality to her but even when she smiled and displayed two lovely rows of teeth, her eyes remained scorched in some distant pain. I couldn't figure this out. It didn't seem to gel with the rest of her. As the twilight melted into dark shadows, she told me her story.

Rita was Chinese-Tibetan, had a broken marriage, a son to look after, and nothing to fall back on. She had left Darjeeling, where she was born and remained till her break-up, and come to Mumbai looking for employment. With her extraordinary beauty and unfortunate circumstances, she was a natural for the oldest profession. Talent scouts, also known as pimps here, pounced on her. After a few chancy encounters, she decided to work from a guesthouse close by, shared by six other girls and a ninety-year-old landlord who, she told me later, was fascinated by her and would spend hours just looking at her in the buff. He would than fall asleep from the exertion in a grandfather armchair.

The guesthouse, a doddering apartment built by the British ages ago, always seemed to eavesdrop, with an inordinate longing, on the opulence of the Taj Mahal Palace Hotel opposite as though, like a blockbuster Hindi film script, they had been siblings separated at birth and one had lost out on all the crockery. With high ceilings, ancient wooden cupboards and lazy fans; pink, flowery wallpaper dripping from the wall in parts and a toilet that leaked like it had never heard of a water shortage, the guesthouse advertised itself as a dancing school. Men came to dance, held the girls close in the dim lights and felt them all over. The girls, who always seemed to run out of clothing at such times, gobbled the tips that rained on them and shrieked in delight. For more action, an outdoor rendezvous had to be fixed.

The dancing school made it very clear that it wasn't a brothel. It was just a meeting point like any other. That way, it escaped unnecessary contact with the law. Of course, the cops visited frequently when they needed human contact or urgent money. The girls paid the landlord a monthly rent and were free to do what they pleased. They could be away for weeks and months on end with customers as long as the dues were paid. Rita, undoubtedly, was the most sought after. Men gave her any amount of money just to spend an evening talking to her. When she walked into the lobby of a good-looking hotel every male eye zeroed in on her like trichologists in a superspecialty clinic looking for dandruff on a piece of chalk.

'I want to have a beer,' she suggested at some point in the conversation. It had got dark and we couldn't keep having tea and biscuits. 'Let's go. I like you.' We got into a cab and left for a nearby watering hole. Rita was a regular here too. She loved her drink and refused to allow me to pay. It was an evening when she wanted to talk.

I sat quietly listening to her endless chatter. Her physical presence did strange things to me, but I kept a discreet distance, trying to look only at her face and listening to the energy of her words. Her long legs were under the table, sometimes they touched mine, her big breasts swayed when she got impassioned, and her bulbous nipples had slipped out of the holds of her bra and were tearing away at her transparent cotton top. Sometimes, tears welled up in her eyes. I could seee that she wanted to talk, and I just kept quiet. I wanted to hold her hands and console her, but I didn't. It wouldn't have stopped with that. It was a tough evening for me as I clutched harder at the bottle of mild beer in my hand.

A few hours into the next day, Rita paid up, staggered to a cab with my support and asked me to come home with her. 'I like you. Make love to me tonight. I won't charge you. Please be with me...' I was frightened. I told her, stammering and nervous, that my parents would be waiting for me and I had to go home. I dropped her at her digs and went home to broken slumber.

Rita and I met often after that. We became good friends. She was making a lot of money and loved spending it on me. She introduced me to her friends and fed me details about her life and work. She had an amazing variety of customers from all over the world, several very well positioned in life. They would take her on long business trips to various parts of India. Rita had also moved on to her second heavily stamped passport.

We would visit the innumerable booze dens spread all over the city, sneakily tucked away in corridors of buildings wasting away, just like those who found comfort in them. These were dives, cheap and worn out, cleaved out of amorphous trunks of real estate and illegally leased out. Wizened, gnarled hands boiled eggs, cleaned the broken tables and served the booze. No questions were asked. But you could discuss anything. Not a soul would bother to listen in. There were no arguments that led to fights or shootouts.

Everyone looked at Rita with admiration, then sighed and gulped a very large peg neat. Not one person in the overcrowded dives ever tried to touch her or pass an uncomplimentary remark. I was nervous in the beginning, wondering how I would protect her from those who wanted to feast on her body. They knew that she was a hooker and would be available for a price. She also dressed with abandon and was sometimes the only woman in the dives. But they understood the pain that inhabited her soul because it was the same pain that relentlessly tortured them. They shared the rack. It is not easy to belong to the flesh trade. It isn't easy either to drink oneself silly day in and day out and live on the margins of the boulevard. They were all trying to shake off the beast. Yet, even when they were seemingly out of the clutches of temperance, they maintained a hold on themselves. Not once, in years, was Rita ever heckled. The dives were packed all the time with a desperate restlessness. They attracted the underside of Mumbai. One genuine police raid and all the petty thieves in the city would be in the net.

Rita loved to drink. And when she drank, she talked even more. She told me about her lovers, the places she visited and the money she made, which was considerably more than what I would ever earn from a lifetime of selling words. She often told me that I was her only friend. 'I am lonely,' she would say. 'Very lonely. Every man wants my body. Let them take it. I don't care. It doesn't bother me now. I have given it to everybody. But you are my only friend in the world.'

Our friendship (which remained platonic, but with difficulty!) lasted close to two decades. Rita is still as delectable as apples in spring, and her body still alive with the agitation of passion. Recently, I took her for an HIV test. Rita tested negative. She tested again because we couldn't believe it, and again she was negative. I spoke to the doctor and asked him to confirm the result. She tested negative a third time.

We were ecstatic. It was a miracle. Rita had spent her entire life servicing men for a livelihood and had rarely used a condom. She had a multinational, multicultural, widely travelled clientele with a wide repertoire of sexual quirks. Conservative estimates swear that Mumbai is India's HIV/AIDS capital, that India arguably has more HIV cases than any other country in the world. In a country of over a billion people with complex sexual mores, Rita, Colaba's most sought-after consort, still remained untouched by the insidious virus that had claimed millions of lives.

That evening, shocked, unbelieving, and hoping to make amends for a past that she could do nothing about now, Rita took me to the city's oldest cathedral, adjacent to Flora Fountain. We entered just before the guard shut the gates, signed the guest book and seated ourselves on a wooden bench in the back rows. The high white ceiling, clean and glistening in a new coat of paint, and the huge cross on the wall right ahead, looked at us with compassion. Jesus Christ had died for us sinners, Rita insisted. Barefoot in crimson nail polish and on her beautiful knees now, she held my hand in its moist softness. She was certain that He had saved her. We held hands and prayed together.

We picked up the Bible from the bench, opened a page at random and read Psalm 51:

Have mercy upon me, O God, according to Thy loving kindness; according to the greatness of Thy compassion blot out my transgressions.
Wash me thoroughly from my inequity, and cleanse me from my sin, for I am conscious of my transgressions, and my sin is ever in mind.
Purify me with hyssop and I shall be clean; wash me, and I shall be whiter than snow.
Cause me to hear joy and gladness, so that the bones which Thou hast broken may rejoice.
Create in me a clean heart, O God, and renew a steadfast spirit within me.

The cathedral was clothed in silence. Rita wept like a child. She clasped my hand harder and the tears streamed down her frock into the warm folds of her body. The usher silently beckoned that they were shutting for the day and we had to leave. The darkness outside had gathered around the stained-glass windows. A few believers were scattered on the benches, their heads bowed in prayer. We could hear the birds chirping in the garden, and beyond that, from the main road, the drone of life coming to the end of another exhausting day. A gardener was watering the plants and newly introduced guppies were feasting on mosquito larvae in the pond in the garden.

Rita swore that she would never ever have sex again without a condom; she didn't want to have sex at all now if it was without love. She was convinced that Jesus Christ had saved her, convinced that she had been given another go at life, and kept telling me that. In all honesty, I believed her. There was no rational explanation for her negative HIV status. I had been covering HIV and the street for years and several colleagues and friends, who had just rare snatches at high-risk behaviour, had died due to the immune collapse triggered by the virus. And here she was, after a lifetime of living dangerously, still gorgeous and untouched by disease.

Our togetherness, by now, had lapsed into the realm of trauma. She wanted to spend more time with me and I started withdrawing. 'Marry me, live with me,' she pleaded one day. 'I can't live without you. My son has grown up and I have money. I need a man to share my life with. I need you.' Somehow, I couldn't explain anything.

I could see the pain, helplessness and longing in her eyes; they were forever creased in the rubble of loneliness. But I couldn't even begin to say anything in my defence. What could I tell her? How could I ever admit that our friendship only filled the hollows of my own desperation and loneliness in the big city? I was an outsider too: a first-generation immigrant who, like her, was also rootless, homeless and friendless. In the shadows of our friendship, I had only tried to find slices of myself.

In a way, I had also used her.

Ganga is a tall, swarthy, powerfully-built tribal who sells her body at Kala Ghoda. She stands outside a popular art gallery and has a few hundred yards earmarked as her beat. Every streetwalker has an area to herself; sometimes they join forces to secure themselves from police and customer harassment. Rates are fixed all along the street well in advance and lodges prepared for sudden arrivals. A sex worker has to advertise her wares. There is word-of-mouth recommendation that spreads furiously and wide like a virus, but the neighbourhood Ganga works in has a floating population without access to such verbal advertising, however stirring. So she has to doll up. It is her best advertisement.

Ganga wears a saree exposing slices of ample breast, torso and buttock, hangs around the curb and picks up customers at will. She has a large smile plastered on her face in constant welcome. You just can't miss her if she stands on the road. Even if you are headed to the intensive care unit of a hospital and are passing by in an ambulance, you will chance rupturing your neck to look at her twice. Once hooked and negotiations completed, she will hail a cab and take the customer to any of the one-hour hotels littered all over the Fort area. Sometimes, men come in their cars, pick her up, cosy around in the seats and drop her back. They have probably taken the late-night show, worked through the mandatory weekend dinner at the latest eatery, seen the family back home, and decided to go cruising for some action. Ganga has regular customers, too, and like Rita, is much sought after but by a different clientele. She is cheaper and more rustic-looking. All the sex workers know one another but there's no bitching. 'I also have my bag of tricks,' she admits with a mischievous laugh that seems to rise from below her well-padded belly. 'Why do you think the same men return to me for so many years?'

Ganga has a husband and five children. She has never insisted on a condom and has, miraculously again, also escaped the tentacles of the HIV. Her rates are nominal; after twenty years on the beat it is only five hundred rupees for a 'long time'. Most of her clients are middle-aged, middle-class office goers who settle for a quickie before returning home to battered marriages, empty passbooks, leaking rented apartments and the terrifying prospect of having to see through another day without hope.

'I am doing this to support my family,' she tells me. 'Just that. There is no other virtue in what I do. My husband works in the morgue and drinks everyday. He gives me no money. Who will feed the family? Can you give me a job? Will you look after my family? Will you?' Ganga and her large family live on the pavement. They know what she does for a living, but since she is the breadwinner, no questions are asked. Her writ goes unchallenged. Her husband, anyway, was in debt even before she met him. Mangled by life, he had lost all hope. Invaded by untreated drug-resistant lung diseases, he was withering away when Ganga met him. But she had seen enough of life's caprices and survived it all to know that nothing is the end if you decide it isn't in your wily mind. She offered him the straw of a new life. He clutched at it and accepted her as his wife. He was the only man Ganga made love to who didn't pass strictures on her life, and that's when she decided to string him along as her 'mard' (man).

But addiction to cheap alcohol and a litany of failures have extracted all life from him. His movements are slow and deliberate, and his tall and sparse frame seems to inhabit the world of spirits. His waking hours are spent in a daze, and when he hits the cobblestones at night, sleep instantly scythes the demons of his daylight world. Ganga doesn't mind that. She can't explain it, and she doesn't have to, but she says that she loves him to bits. It's a strange love story. Such desire is inexplicable. 'I can never leave him,' she tells me. 'He is my soul. If he is dead, I am dead.' Having seen stray bits of dangerous desire myself, I think I understand her.

Ganga, meanwhile, profits from the night. She is all and more a man could ask for. She takes her customers to tiny rooms with a bed, a fan and a bidet in the corner. The hotels and rooms are old, younger than her profession, of course, but the plaster peels as though the wives and girlfriends of the men who consort with Ganga are crying their hearts out. There is invariably a broken mirror, a bright, leaking plastic bucket, soiled bed sheets, a tap pit-pattering away and dirty cement flooring, broken in parts. Used condoms on the floor, married to semen, add to the patchwork.

These nondescript hotels are big business. There's always a flurry of activity. Taxis, with tinted glasses, thick rexine seat covers, plastic flowers from China, and loud music, like mobile discotheques or boudoirs, come all the way to the entrance. These drops and pick-ups cost a bit more than the normal taxi fares. The driver will tell you what to pay and there's no point arguing with him – it's not the venue to fight over cab fares anyway.

It's all quick, silent and furtive. Couples rush out and are ushered swiftly to rooms. There are several hangers-on. Police raids are common and money has to be paid before the arms of the law reach the rooms. One authentic raid and the 'dhandha' will die for a while. But there are always huge bundles of cash ready and the fat cops know that it doesn't make sense to disrupt their pension plans.

Single women and couples come from everywhere. From discos, dance bars, streets, even from middle-class, respectable homes. These seedy one-hour rooms in even seedier hotels don't cater solely to the hooker. There are educated, office-going couples shopping for a spread of time they can call their own. They too want to love without intrusion and are prepared to spend money for it. Mumbai has a space crunch and how long can copulation be restricted to the rear seats of cabs, dark cinema seats, beaches, family rooms of Irani hotels, desolate street corners and weekend getaways? Ownership of space, however small, is a distant dream for most people in the city and the tiny hotels and their indifferent rooms house several swells of love and longing.

There is also a protracted menu of intoxicants. Drugs, booze and biryani are all on the room-service menu. Monack is the cheapest intoxicant and easily available at all paan shops. It is round and black and rolled in colourful foil; like toffee. One bite and you ride the wings of fantasy. Ganga topped with Monack, and life doesn't seem so bad after all.

Suchitra, a new entrant, is from Meghalaya. She dresses snazzily, smiles loudly, speaks English well and loves to experiment. She is tall, slim and fair with tiny breasts and long legs. On Saturday nights, when disco fever grips the city after a week of hard labour, she wears a red six-inch miniskirt that barely manages to cover her little buttocks, and an equally tiny red top to grab eyes that rove endlessly. Sometimes, the top is so small that the breasts slip out. Then she grins sheepishly and tucks them in again. Of course, she knows that everybody is watching and she loves the attention. It is deliberate, well-directed choreography.

She plasters her face with make-up, smears red paint all over her lips, a little slipping on to the teeth and cheekbones, and gets into unwieldy red stilettos that pinch her toes. A few drinks and a few tokes of brown and she sways in the breeze in her decidedly uncomfortable shoes like a little flower walking into the eye of a tempest. Suchitra is a huge draw.

Her audience is very different. They are not the men who lech at Ganga. They are young, educated, fashionable men with money who just want to have some fun and think nothing about it. She hangs out with them at the Gateway of India, opposite the Taj Mahal Palace hotel, grips their crotches on friendly motorbike rides till they choke, plays with their hormones, and chews on their money. They go to the gym, eat packs of imported protein-enriched powders to enhance their muscles, and fashion their hair after David Beckham. They don't smoke hashish with her, and always use condoms. But Suchitra is great fun. She is also a sex junkie. They can't resist her. You can do anything to her; even thrash her violently, and she will consider it a favour.

Suchitra is only seventeen. She is already married and divorced with a child. There are so many like her. Beautiful young girls from all over India destroyed by domestic violence or deceived by love. When the dream dies, they are already full with another life, and it is too late. Unwanted, unloved, abandoned, it's the same old story. The cast and the locations change. That's all. Come to Mumbai and sell your body. You will never starve.

Suchitra's protectors include the local drug mafia. She is now chasing brown; she's hooked on it. She has lost weight, has strange rashes on her skin, isn't choosy about whom she sleeps with any more, doesn't use protection, has had several abortions and has even given up dressing to the hilt. She still has that endearing smile, but the eyes are glassy, lost and unfocused. All she needs is three hundred rupees a day for her drug habit. It is expensive. If she doesn't get her fix, the withdrawal symptoms are horrendous. She gets crazed and will do anything for it.

'So what, I will die... Let me die... Why should I live...? To be fucked by everybody... That's what they want.... Nothing else... Who cares??? I don't care. I have nothing to live for,' she cries. Several social workers have tried to rescue her. Even her mother came to Mumbai and dragged her home. But Suchitra ran back. At some point, somewhere, something snapped forever inside her. The discord with her family grew stretch marks that bled. It couldn't be bridged even in the most accommodating crevices of her mind, and she retreated into her shell, like a snail, reclusive and alone, in abnegation. Within it, like an embryo that was feeding on itself, she was left to nourish idle and ruinous fantasies. All she wants now is to run headlong into the arms of an abyss, and float in its clouds forever.

She sits by the Gateway of India every night. The sea lashes away, sometimes in inexplicable pain, sometimes in glee, but always with enthusiasm. The moon is a little crescent far away. Even when it gets bigger it is still beyond her reach. Suchitra unfolds a silver foil, packs the brown powder into it and lights matchstick after matchstick under the foil as she desperately chases the powder. It is all over in fifteen minutes. Sometimes, she sits with her group, hungry for escape, and they share the needle. Her soft, olive skin is riddled with tiny marks. The sea tears away, the tide rushes in, and the young bucks of Saturday night are riding their hormones towards her on 500 cc horsepower. 'Come fuck me,' she screams. 'Just fuck me. Hard. Hard. Hard. Hard.'

The Taj Mahal Palace hotel is lit up like a Christmas tree, the old residential area of Electric House is slumbering, the little lanes of Colaba are tired of the day's hustle, deckhands snore on gently swaying merchant boats tethered to the promenade, and even the mangy street dogs are curled up next to malnourished, naked children on the pavement. It has been another vicious day. The party people have also gone home. The night is long and dark and hollow. Suchitra's words spill headlong into its bottomless pit splaying the morning with diseased seed.

'Just call me Bernie,' she says flatly. It's easy, but I don't take the call. I may have a lot to lose. I turn around to see a foreigner, a white woman, in a black T-shirt, jeans and pumps leaning against the wall. We are in Colaba, in one of the lanes close to the causeway. It's late in the evening and I can make out a bit more than her silhouette in the shadows. 'Why should I even call you?' I retort. She laughs. 'That's a good one.' We laugh together.

Bernie asks for a light. I can see the gambit. 'Let's have a drink instead,' I suggest. We go to a bar felons have easy access to. A couple of neat rums later, Bernie is as excited as one who has just learnt to speak. 'I live in England now,' she tells me in an accent as tough as Muhammad Ali. 'But I am from New Zealand. Met an Englishman on holiday, upped and joined him in Richmond. I got pregnant. I didn't know that he was an arms dealer. The law caught up with him. I got jailed as an accomplice. I aborted, was released after a muted sentence, got seriously depressed and sought crack. I have been travelling for almost a year, been in India four months. Manali, Goa, Kerala, but I like it here in Mumbai. It is so free and easygoing. Can I have one more drink?' So many lies... After all this, I wonder if I can ever trust anyone. On the street, the truth is the first casualty. It gets devoured in no time. It is easy meat.

Another large rum wiped neat, and it's time to take a good look at this strange woman who now believes that I am her analyst. Another hour of this and she may take me home. Or I may just crack up. Not choices I am ridiculously crazy about.

Unlike other junkies on the road, Bernie is filled out. She is a large, tall woman with silky blonde hair and blue-green eyes. She is in her thirties with a tarantula's web around her eyes and a thin, cruel and unfeeling mouth. Bernie lives in Colaba, in one of the dugouts infested by Mumbai's famed bandicoots costing a few hundred rupees a night. She is a heroin addict and sex worker. She also has a local pimp who gets her customers. Colaba has an organized racket of white sex workers, but Bernie doesn't want any of it. I say 'white' sex workers because there are no 'black' women in the trade. There are loads of Africans but they are into drugs and smuggling. They have been in Colaba for years and even the stray dogs recognize them now. They are as real as the municipal rubble.

Bernie prefers to work it alone with her pimp. 'Babu is a sweet chap,' she tells me. 'He knows everybody in Mumbai. I charge five thousand rupees for the night and he takes a thousand. I am very good. I can do many things. You wanna try? He gets me so many young boys. They come in their cars, rich kids with rich daddies, and take me to hotels and discos and their farmhouses. It's great. I love it here. One of them even wants to marry me, but he is really too young, still in high school. He wants to marry me and come to England. He says his dad has a lot of money and he will even buy me a house in Kensington. Actually, they all want to marry me. Even Babu. Do you want to marry me?'

Bernie checked into Colaba straight from the airport. *Lonely Planet* told her, quite rightly, that it was a cool place to hang out in. Colaba zooms in on you if you are a single white woman. Babu fixed it all up in a jiffy. He is the local pimp and is well-connected to all the hotel managers. They tell him about new residents and their respective requirements.

Babu fixes everything. He knows where to get the booze and the drugs, and whom to pay what and how much. He even hires long-distance cabs, gets airport tickets and changes currency at rates much higher than what the banks allow. He knows what every nationality wants, speaks several languages, and also knows Goa well. The Mumbai-Goa trade link is very profitable. He has been doing this for years and so must be good at it. He also has the local policemen in his employ. Everything happens in the stealth of bright sunshine and yet remains hidden. If a baby crawled around Colaba it would think it is as dangerous as its crib.

Babu has short hair and a thick moustache, is heavily tattooed with trinkets and earrings. His eyes are lined in 'kajal' and appear droopy, but that's just a decoy. He misses nothing. He will pass an ophthalmologist's test a furlong away. 'Tell me what you want,' he asks me in street lingo, dragging every word with a wheelbarrow. He doesn't look into my eyes, he is always looking away, behind me and around me, but he knows that something is amiss and that I don't belong there. He's way too smart to miss a trap. He is the king of con.

'You want boys,' he asks 'or girls?'

'You want drugs? Which one, how much, when, where? Scared of police, don't worry. I am there. How much you pay? You want Bernie? Not today, tomorrow.'

We decide to have a cup of tea from the chai boys on cycles on the promenade. 'Tell what you want,' pushes Babu. 'Too much talking, you, no good, tell fast.' I tell him that I want to talk to Bernie alone. He doesn't allow it. 'Why talk to Bernie alone? Talk to Bernie now. What you want to know? Ask me. I fix her up for you. Or give me five hundred rupees and I go.'

'Yes, give him five hundred,' pipes in Bernie, raising her voice, screaming loudly, her eyes blazing in anger. 'If you want to talk to me alone, do that. Babu is my manager and I do whatever he tells me.'

I can't take this anymore. They are both freaked out psychos. They are creating a scene, people are watching us and I am making no ground. I am getting impatient. But I also know that I can't lose my cool. It will ruin everything. Babu tugs at my shirtsleeves and I hate that. I get claustrophobic if anyone touches me on the street. I admonish him with a hard stare but he keeps at it. I have to leave now before I blow up. 'See you tomorrow,' I say hurriedly and rush off. 'Same place. Bye.'

'Give some money,' they scream together after me. 'At least five hundred rupees.'

I walk away, cross the road, cross another to spoil a tail if there is one, and jump into a cab. I have had enough of Colaba for the night.

Weeks later, I am playing volleyball in one of the swanky clubs in Mumbai. A large woman in a black one-piece swimsuit emerges from the pool, hooks on to a young fellow in the volleyball team and they go to the changing rooms together. It is Bernie. I just can't believe it. I stand and stare. She sees me, and smiles with those blue-green eyes under her crow's feet. Her cruel mouth is impassive.

'Just call me Bernie,' she tells him softly, linking hands. They have turned the corner and have disappeared.

Tenrik is not more than thirteen. Small, gentle with a sweet face and an athletic, lithe frame, he smiles a lot. He hangs around the Gateway of India and then slips into the folds of the promenade imperceptibly. He is always in clean white shirts, black cotton slacks and formal black shoes. He even wears clean, matching socks.

Tenrik is from Manipur. He ran away from home looking for a job and landed up in Colaba. The touts soon sniffed him out and he is now part of a group of male sex workers. They are all young boys and have had sexual experiences as little children. Times have changed and the pimps don't just sell girls anymore. Boys are added to the bedspread.

The sex trade in little boys is thriving. There are Indian customers as well as those who come from the Gulf countries and the West. The boys are runaways and haven't been to school, but are now as canny as gazelles in the Masai Mara. They can spot a customer like a lizard sighting a fly on the wall, can converse in good English, are well paid, and have become confident men of the world.

In India, if you are a male, it is easier to travel with a companion of the same sex. No questions are asked and no eyebrows are raised while checking into hotels. If the partner is of the opposite gender and the legality of the relationship in some doubt, every male and his distant cousin will ask for a slice of the action. And if your partner is a foreigner, male or female, every shred of morality, so easily donned when convenient, will be dumped into the bin. You will be harangued. The cops will also raid and extract money because you are vulnerable to blackmail.

Tenrik has it relatively easy because he always travels with someone of the same sex. While the Gateway is a famous gay cruising spot and open to every class of society, Tenrik and the others pick out only wealthy customers. They like to be wined and dined and taken to Goa and other fun locales. Tenrik has been everywhere, even overseas. He has a bank account and lives and spends as dangerously as he loves. He says he prefers white foreigners. 'They are very decent and kind and pay a lot. They don't force you to do anything.'

Maithili and Simi are cross-dressers. They are male. Maithili is Mohan and Simi is Suresh. But they are men locked in women's bodies. So they give themselves women's names and identities and dress up in skirts, tank tops, falsies, and sway their padded hips on high-heeled shoes. They are heavily made up and wear wigs and gaudy lipstick. Their gestures, mannerisms and voice, project melodramatic femininity. They believe that they are walking billboards of estrogen. They will do anything to be noticed. They also hang around the Gateway and have their sets of customers. Tenrik is not part of this. He belongs to the upper echelons of male prostitution. 'Chhee,' he says when I ask him about them. 'They are cheap.'

Tenrik makes the effort to chat me up. I am sitting alone on the promenade and he eyes me with intent. I know what's coming, and the old ruse, 'Let's have a drink,' always works. He has tiny eyes, and a clean, sophisticated air about him. His hair is cut short with a side parting and gelled nicely. He has a sharp profile and is well-boned. He will grow up into a very attractive man. He wears the look of the young rake with aplomb. Instinctively, I decide to take him to a five-star hotel. He isn't surprised. It's obvious that he is used to this.

We take positions at the only table available in the far corner facing the entrance, place the order and begin talking. Tenrik thinks I have a room in the hotel and believes that his prospects for the evening are excellent. He tells me about his home and family. He has been in Mumbai for three years.

He says he is fifteen but that's certainly an exaggeration. The coffee shop is packed. We are through with the second beer and I see him looking around nervously. 'What's the matter,' I ask. 'Nothing,' he assures me. But I know something is wrong.

'Look at that man,' he eventually tells me, pointing to a colourfully dressed big-made gent with thick dyed sideburns on a largely balding pate a few tables away. 'I go to him every week. He spends a lot of money on me.' The man he points out is with an equally large woman and grown-up girls. 'That's his family,' Tenrik continues. 'His wife knows about me and doesn't mind. She has a lover.' He then points out several others. They are all his customers, he claims.

I ask him why he does it. Is the pain, and the fear of disease, really worth it? He tells me that he makes a lot of money, and that he loves getting buggered. 'I love sex. I will do anything for it.' What about condoms? 'If the customers are keen on it, I don't mind. I know about AIDS and all that. Are you going to lecture me? I have heard enough of AIDS. I am not frightened of death. We all have to go one day. When it is my time, I will also go.'

We finish off and make for the exit. I tell him that I have to leave for home. He is disappointed, thanks me for the drinks, shakes my hand, and returns to the coffee shop.

He always sits on the part of the promenade next to the Radio Club. It is not far from the entrance to the Taj Mahal Palace Hotel, and is always hosting some party or the other. Cheap boarding houses spill out of the road opposite, and the only bisexual bar in the locality is less than a hundred yards away. There is always a stream of variegated human traffic. In several ways, it is a great place to hang out.

He is normally there in the evenings, just before the sun sets in a golden haze. It is the time offices shut and people throng the Gateway for a last glimpse of the sea and the breeze before jumping into packed suburban trains. But he is in no rush.

He is scrubbed clean, well-groomed and his clothes are well-stitched. He wears a thick gold chain with a pendant in the shape

70

of a lion attached to it, a bracelet, emerald earrings and even a gold nipple ring that is always visible because his shirt is open till the navel. He also displays a clean and taut torso. He lives in the distant suburbs, spends the day sleeping, working out in the gym, visits the parlour and then catches a train to the southern end of the city for his work shift that begins around sunset and can extend for days depending on the assignment. He is a cocky young man, stands out from the crowd in a fashion, and reeks of the seductive fragrance of musk.

Salim is a gigolo, and a very successful one at that. We met several times on the promenade. I introduced myself and got him to talk. In a few weeks, we became buddies. He also explained his work in detail. 'It's very easy,' he says. 'There are so many women here looking for action. There are travellers, local women, married, single, divorced, widowed or just bored. There are all kinds. Everyone wants someone to talk to and be escorted to parties, picnics and different cities if they are travellers. It can be just friendship, but it often develops into more. Men too want the same things. They are more aggressive about it, that's all.'

He tells me that it is big business all over the city. The promenade alone has several gigolos. They operate individually, never in groups. Huge gigolo egos are always in collision course in company. Salim is a bisexual gigolo and is always in demand. Saturday nights are gay nights in the disco down the road. He never misses it. The entrance fee is fat but he makes fantastic amounts that night. For the owner, the likes of Salim in his disco are good for business and he is always welcomed with a smile. The entrance fee is also waived sometimes. 'The sex is also great,' he says. 'Come there with me and see what happens. You will be blown out of your mind.'

I accept and the next Saturday I pay the fat entrance fee and enter the disco. I go alone, not with Salim. It is a rip-off. There are no free drinks and everything on the menu is far too exorbitant. 1

can't afford anything. But the disco is rich in energy and experience. The music is choppy and the dance floor is packed with men sizing one another up. Women sit on the mezzanine floor waiting for customers.

It is a small disco. The walls are painted in fluorescent colours. After you have picked up someone, you step away from the dance floor and walk into an alcove at a lower level, on the way to the toilet, where there is some privacy. After the initial groping in semi-darkness you decide if you want to make a larger investment in time, money and pleasure. The clientele is well-heeled – there are personnel from docked ships and airlines passing through, backpackers, and people in the entertainment business.

I walk up to the mezzanine floor, order a beer and watch it all. Salim is nowhere to be seen. He is probably booked for the night. Scores of women look me up. I could be in a glitzy fashion show anywhere in the world. The dim lights don't reveal much but I can make out that the women are gorgeous and immaculately attired. I begin to feel like an urchin in my customary track pants and pumps. I self-consciously slap some order to my unruly mop of hair, adjust my shirt, take out my handkerchief and wipe some grime off my face. I have had a long day in the humidity. Across me, and staring with curiosity, is a beautiful woman. I try to chat her up but she brushes me off coldly and tells me with some degree of arrogance that it will cost me five thousand rupees to spend even a little time with her. She also tells me that it is a good deal for me, a real bargain, because business is down. Why, I ask, surprised. The place is packed. Business must be good.

'You don't understand,' she says. 'You must be new here. The men want men. They don't want us anymore. So you have a very good deal. I never charge less than ten thousand rupees.' If men go to both genders, there will be other issues. I ask her about AIDS and she tells me that she is no fool and will never sleep with a man who doesn't use a condom. 'I also look at their bodies. If they have scars or look sick I back off. I don't want to die. My son is in boarding school. I love life and have a great time. I don't want to die because of silly sex.' Her English is excellent and her clothes are straight off a pret line. She is also attractive in a very Indian way. 'If you are so broke, at least buy me a beer,' she adds as an afterthought. 'Why should I talk to you for nothing. The only reason I answered your stupid questions is because you speak English well.' I oblige and we toast to good times.

Manisha is in her thirties and has done well for herself, if high earnings are the sole criterion for success. She was married early in a small town and was soon divorced. She didn't want to go back to her parents' home and came to Mumbai with her young son. She had a degree in economics but that wasn't enough for her to get a good job. She was brought up in comfort and didn't feel like scrounging for a living just because she was a single mother. She rented a small apartment, admitted her son in school, and took up an office job that didn't pay too much. It wasn't easy making ends meet in the big city and she was wondering what to do. She didn't want to get married again either. The long commute to work and the never-ending bills at her doorstep literally raised her blood pressure. Then one day her prayers were answered.

'I used to come to the Gateway in the evenings to chill out. I used to sit on the promenade, watch the sea and wonder what to do. I couldn't go on living like this. I am ambitious. I want a good life. You live only once and so why suffer?' she tells me softly, washing her words with the beer. Then she met a man who said that he had been following her for weeks and had a proposition for her if she was interested. He said that she had the attitude and the profile to move in the right circles and promised to connect her, for a commission, with the people that mattered in the city. Manisha gave it a thought and agreed with the terms on offer.

'I had no choice really,' she tells me. 'I just couldn't continue with the boring middle-class life I was leading. I had to do something, anything. I tried going to Dubai and Muscat but I didn't get the right openings. Time was also passing me by and I was scared of ending up an old, tired and poor woman. So I just said yes to him. There are no regrets. I have clients now, all rich, healthy and good-looking. Money buys everything. It also buys looks. It is God. I have a lot of money now. Get me another beer.'

She orders me easily, with impudence, as though I am her orderly. If she has so much money, why should I get the beer? I don't argue, though, and hold myself from retaliating. It is my investment to write a book, I tell myself gently, and take several deep, yogic breaths to control my rising anger. I count to ten slowly like they instruct in all the stress-management books.

We talk for over an hour. After several beers, which I pay for and which leaves very little in my pocket for the return journey home, Manisha gives me her numbers and asks me to contact her because she thinks I am 'educated, decent and can talk sense'. I am flattered. She sights an old customer who gestures to her from across the room, kisses me on the cheek and pushes off, waving from the door and signalling to call her soon. I get in touch a few days later and we meet at a Barista in town, near the Regal cinema. This time, thankfully, she agrees to pay. Manisha has exquisite manners, is refined, is never an embarrassment in public and has the right connections. I like her in the daylight, away from the psychedelic innuendos of the bisexual bar. She also has a lot of confidence and knows her mind. She dresses well, is driven around and tells me that she has acquired a fancy apartment costing crores of rupees in a swanky high-rise. She is happy to be where she is. She doesn't need the greasy disco but she enjoys it and drops by when she can. She scouts new talent – it's like keeping an ear on the ground – and her voyeuristic instincts are fed.

I find her fascinating and she admits that she doesn't mind hanging around with me because I am not a 'threat', whatever that means. She takes me under her wing and offers to set me up in life 'big time' if I am interested. 'You will be driving a Mercedes and not jumping into a train like this. Look at your clothes; silly track pants. You don't even have a proper hair cut. What do you earn? Peanuts? I bet you are renting a dirty little room far into the suburbs. What do you think all these people with money are doing? How do you think they make money? You think they are intelligent and educated? Rubbish. There are certain things to be done. That's all. I will tell you what to do. We can be partners. I know everybody. I have made money. You are a pleasant and intelligent fellow. Use your brains, don't be so naive. I was also like you once upon a time wondering about right and wrong and such nonsense. When you have money in your pocket, wrong automatically becomes right.'

She invites me, several meetings later, to a terrace party in one of the more affluent parts of Mumbai. The party goes on for two days and two nights. People come and go as they please. Even the water is served in sterling silver. The apartment facing the sea is as large as a hockey stadium. There is a golden fountain in the living room, and priceless antiquities and paintings are carelessly strewn all around. Couples enter and exit rooms. Everyone is being swapped. The food, drink and ambience are a delight. I have travelled a bit and prided myself on having tasted bites of opulence in some of the more exotic spaces of the globe. But all this is truly startling. Wealth is being bandied about in an extravagant mix of refinement and obscenity. And what's worse, the hungry and the homeless live on the street several floors below.

I huddle in a dark corner alone, clearly unsettled by what I see. I just don't belong. Manisha is also lost. She is busy networking in some ornate room somewhere in this huge apartment. Not in any mood to seek out company, I have a few drinks and then go to the bathroom but think twice before washing my hands. The bathroom fittings glisten in gold and appear far too complicated for the simple purpose of ejecting a stream of water. So I wipe my hands with my handkerchief and swipe them clean on the lush bathroom towels, which is much easier than opening a tap, check if I haven't messed up anything, look around for cameras in case I have been caught in the act, and run out of the bathroom for more beer from a silver container. That seems the easiest thing to do. It also frees me from the concerns of worrying about etiquette.

I go back to my corner and look around. I recognize several people who are regularly featured in the society pages of newspapers. They are the movers and shakers of the city. They run industry, media, fashion, real estate and enterprise. 'Are they all in the game?' I whisper to Manisha when she returns from her capers. 'You are such an idiot,' she retorts. 'In which world are you living? Of course.'

A few weeks later my eyes almost fall out.

Manisha is featured in the society pages as an accomplished woman who is making waves in the city. Along with her is the poster boy of emerging India. They are holding hands and kissing one another in the air. She looks resplendent in red and gold.

Maybe, I should give her a call. Maybe, I shouldn't.

I don't know.

I visit the disco for months on end. There are several newcomers but Manisha isn't there. I decide against calling her. I have nothing new to tell her. I bump into Salim one day, after a long time. We greet each other heartily. He hugs me tight and slaps me on the back several times. His shirt is sill unbuttoned till the navel, prominently displaying the gold nipple ring. He wears a rich tan, looks lean and well-muscled, and seems very pleased with himself. He tells me that he has been holidaying in Mauritius and is now off to South Africa for a month. He also introduces me to Stella, his sponsor.

It is not dark yet and we are still on the road in Colaba, near the Shiv temple. But Stella is in tight blue denim pants so low that I can make out the dark traces of her pubis. Another step, I tell myself, and it will fall off. I wouldn't mind that, and stare hopefully. She tops it with a richly crafted bra with tiny mirrors and lace, softened by cascading golden locks, that barely cover her nipple rings and pert breasts. A giant lapis with its pyrite trimmings glistens on her belly button.

'Have fun,' I tell Salim with undisguised envy. I try not to hate him. He smiles and winks. The two walk arm-in-arm into the maze of shops and passers-by. He squeezes her taut, barely covered buttocks. His fingers sink inside her pants into her soft flesh. They also stray a bit between her legs and wander around. She draws closer. I just stand and stare and watch the crowds and the failing light swallow them in no time.

CHAPTER 4

ASHA DAN

Did'st Thou give me this inescapable loneliness so that it would be easier for me to give Thee all?

—Dag Hammarskjold

In the late eighties, a friend and I spent the long monsoon months picking up homeless and abandoned people from the streets of Mumbai. Despite the chronic shortage of green cover, the island city gets pockmarked by the rains and is flattened year after year. Houses collapse, thousands die or are rendered homeless, epidemics run their course and, yet, for some inexplicable reason, more trees are hacked to death and more steel and concrete spirals upwards towards the sky after the rains have let up. It is any city's nightmare and every builder's dream. Matchbox-size homes cost fortunes, and people go to any lengths to acquire even a rickety roof over their heads. After the floods, there will also be no water in the taps!

Along with my friend, an experienced hand at rescue work, I scoured abandoned buildings, porticos, verandahs, stairwells, any covered space, even open umbrellas and plastic cloth stretched between branches of trees, to seek out the city's huge numbers of homeless people. We wore gumboots and raincoats, and carried flashlights, some money and first aid. Most of those who needed aid were old, desolate, sick and dying. They had been discarded by families, had given up hope, and were slowly being taken over by diseases that were within striking range of the last glow of life. Their immune systems had packed up and germs swarmed all over for the kill.

They saw through the pain with cheap alcohol and drugs and sometimes clung to one another for hope and warmth; it was the last gasp of the dying and the dispossessed. Sometimes, street dogs sat with them through their last rites and shed a tear when their master died. Then they moved on to another shelter and stayed with their new owners till the end. The canine instinct for survival was much stronger; their minds not chafed by the pain of abandonment. All they missed out on was a good meal. Then they sought garbage dumps and friendly kitchens and when the sun finally came out, shook themselves dry and romped off towards better times.

Death is never as easy as one imagines it to be. Neither does it come readily; it is never on time. Sometimes, it is an early visitor. You don't want it, you hate the knock on the door and do all you can to keep it away. But it has its own mind, and will do what it will. On the street, it can arrive too late. You can die just waiting for it. The moments before the final release are long and painful. When you are in a wet gutter with rats feeding off your rotten flesh and with maggots gouging out your eyes, even hope gives up on you. There is no money to buy that last drink. There is not enough strength to commit murder; even suicides fail. All one can do is to lie back and wait to die. It's a long, interminable wait for the last nail.

We found scores of human bodies waiting to die in every locality. They just begged to be delivered from this life. We picked them up

in hired cabs and took them to Asha Dan, Mother Teresa's home
for the dispossessed, in Byculla, Central Mumbai.

The hospice is always full. Every bed is occupied. The facilities
are managed by petite, smiling young sisters, most of them from
Kerala. Several hours of daily prayer have empowered them to
love without restraint. They have a profound belief in their calling
and see the Lord Jesus Christ in the sick and the dying, and in the
hurt and the pain that never seems to char their ready smiles. The
sisters are goaded by the desire to serve. It's the Lord's will, they say
happily. In their love for all life, they have also unwittingly roped
in the Buddha's Fourth Noble Truth, which teaches right intention
as the second step in the eight-fold path. It says: *Cause no harm,
and treat yourself and others with loving kindness and compassion while
seeking true happiness, that which comes from being free from grasping
and clinging.* In the *Majjhima Nikaya Sutta*, 'The Dog-Duty Ascetic,'
the Buddha describes how 'bright intentions lead to bright results'.
It is the path to deliverance. In their simplicity and unflinching
faith in Jesus Christ, the sisters were living the Buddha's words.

The emaciated bodies were gladly picked up, bathed and fed.
Long, thin white worms eagerly crawled out of washed and still
wasting bodies. The sisters, smiling and agile in their white sarees
with blue borders, picked them one by one, gently, without causing
pain, and dumped them into large trays. They then lovingly wiped
the dying bodies in gauze dipped in antiseptic. They joked, laughed,
pulled their cheeks, dressed them in warm clothing and made
them feel loved and wanted. No questions were asked. They were
abandoned and the street was their address. The Missionaries of
Charity needed no other recommendation.

They had entered the zone, the final frontier of mindlessness.
Nothing mattered now. Death came to them everyday like wafts
of breeze. It teased and taunted them like feathers grazing their

nostrils, and then carelessly sauntered away. They clutched at it, cajoled it to stay, begged of it to remain with them. But the fragrance of death only offered a fleeting kiss and woke them to the world of the living. Some recovered, most of them slipped into deep delirium from which they never returned. But when they died, it was with dignity, smiling, washed and clean, their wounds and souls fed. They were given a burial befitting those who had carried the cross on crutches.

Asha Dan, in the midst of it all, has seen a lot. It is home to offerings that even the street can't hold with both hands. But when Haseena Banoo was brought to the hospice, the excitement was palpable. Every resident had had more than a large helping of the crumbs of life, but it was certainly the first time that an eleven-year-old sex worker and drug addict had entered their lives. Barely five feet in her calloused feet, gaunt, ebony-skinned and talkative, with a smile playing in her eyes, Haseena was rescued from Kamathipura by members of a film unit who chanced upon her while shooting a documentary on drug addiction. They took her to Bhatia Hospital in the vicinity to be detoxified and then brought her to Asha Dan to be rehabilitated.

The early days were difficult. Haseena had many adjustments to make. This wild child of nature had to be cultured. The discipline of the hospice was hard to take. There were fixed hours for meals, a bath every day was necessary, medicines had to be taken without argument and, most important, recreational drugs were taboo. She had to make new friends from circumstances that were alien to her. She had to rein in her ways and belong to a regimen that sought sanity and order as its commandments.

The strict regimen worked well for her. She put on weight soon, wore nice clothes, was clean and scrubbed at all times, and endeared herself to the others with her glib tongue. With time, she settled well into the tenor of everyday life at Asha Dan. One eye, though, was always placed on the large blue gates that barricaded her from the illusory world of Pehli Galli in Kamathipura, just a hop and skip away, where drugs, sex and money were strewn around like confetti. Haseena would have loved to slip back to that world of chance. But, for now, her painful past was consigned to the last chips of memory.

Haseena's story is the theme song of lust and betrayal on the streets. Born to a poor Muslim family in south India, Haseena's father died early. The large family of four brothers and three sisters, and several half-siblings, now left to the whims of another breadwinner, slowly slithered into further penury. An uncle convinced her mother that he would find a job for the child in Mumbai and whisked her away to the brothels of Kamathipura.

For two years, Haseena was tortured, raped and sold several times for profit. Surekha, a drug peddler and addict, then picked her up and used her as an easy conduit for drugs. She became her employer. Both gained in the relationship. Haseena got the drugs she needed and Surekha a larger clientele. The bond grew. They realized that they needed one another. A complex network of circumstances ensured that.

This relationship, despite its commercial utility to both, also remained suspended in the intense need to belong. They had plumbed the recesses of each other's needs. Nothing and no one on the street needed them in any way. But they had each other, however incomprehensible the alliance. Haseena even had Surekha's name tattooed on the inside of her right hand. Like creepers sharing the compound wall, they fed off each other.

A young, unwed mother, Surekha used to pick up girls between the ages of nine and fifteen and introduce them to brown sugar. Once hooked, an addict will do anything for the next fix. She then threw her young wards to the junkies and sadists who thronged Arab Gully and made a living. If the girls refused sex, their next toke was held back. So they gave in. The withdrawal symptoms were horrendous and the girls would do anything to escape it. It was good business.

'Everybody takes drugs there,' says Haseena innocently about Kamathipura. 'Even little children.' She recalls her first chase of brown. She was feeling ill and Surekha promised her some medicine. The remedy offered was a seemingly harmless shot of heroin. But it was the beginning of an unending demonic journey into the convulsions of despair. She wanted more. If she didn't get the 'medicine', she felt sick. She was given more of it in small, measured drips.

The thin girl grew gaunt and stretched and hollowed. Her arms and legs sprouted marks with all the needles pinched into them. When there was no space there, she shot the whites of her eyes. They are dark and dead now, like hollows in her face, but come alive suddenly and shine like marbles when she consorts with a new idea. Then they dazzle.

All blood seemed to have been drained from her body by a suction pump. She knew that all she had to do for her next fix was to spread her emaciated legs. Free sex had easy takers, and the heroin numbed all feeling. She grew to be a sex junkie. She was dependent on sex and brown sugar and needed a steady supply of both. Any withdrawal prompted manic reactions. 'Look at me now,' says Haseena. 'I was so plump and beautiful before. Now, after so many months of brown sugar, I am so thin. I didn't even know what I was taking. I thought it was medicine.' When she was rescued, Haseena's dark, blotched skin stretched tight over her bones like a well-fitting mask. There was no flesh: just skin, bones and some blood and a desire to live for more self-destruction.

'I will never touch brown again,' she swears. She kisses the pendant of Jesus Christ pinned to her frock and explains that though she is a Muslim she also likes Jesus. Religion is also thrown about randomly on the streets. It is used to great advantage by political parties. No one understands it but the hopelessness is so great that any straw in the wind is taken for a sign of deliverance. Anything may work, and sometimes it does.

Haseena talks of her friends from the street. One of them, Deepa, was an extra in films. 'She had lots of money and was so beautiful. She used to change her clothes five times a day. She took brown sugar and died. I cried so much. She was my best friend.'

There were other horror stories. Chanda was murdered because she didn't agree to sleep with the man she disliked, Jyoti was raped everyday for weeks because she spat on the face of her pimp, Latha delivered a baby girl on the street and sold her immediately for a shot of heroin, and Zeenat's arms were cut off from the shoulders to make her a professional beggar. Rehana was crippled with acid thrown on her for fun. They were all the same age. She also remembers the police. 'They take money from everybody. If you don't pay, they hit you. They even rape you. They stop at nothing.'

She tells me about the 'first time'. Every detail is embedded in her soul. They can never be exorcized as long as she lives. Saleem, a local thug, raped her on the street. She was sleeping when he gagged and assaulted her. He took her to one of the 'addas' (places) in Falkland Road near Kamathipura where she passed out. She must have been about nine then. She then got hooked on brown and all subsequent sexual assaults were inured. She realized that her body could easily be bartered for ice creams, trinkets and pretty clothes. 'Whenever I wanted something, I just slept with someone,' she says without remorse. 'It was so easy.'

What does Haseena want to do now? 'I want to study hard and help the poor. I want the others to stop taking drugs. I am sure they will listen. So what if I am small?' She also wants to learn English and talk like Peter Taylor, the steward from British Airways, who used to help out at Asha Dan whenever he was in Mumbai. She likes his style and accent. She also likes his fair skin, light eyes and golden hair. She tries to imitate him, and laughs at herself after a few futile attempts.

'Haseena is a problem,' confess the sisters at Asha Dan. 'She is stubborn, doesn't want to take her medicines, doesn't have a bath until she is forced to, and is forever trying to run away. She is always sweet-talking someone or the other into opening the gates for her. Asha Dan has had other drug cases. But never one so young or so defiant.'

When the sisters are not looking, Haseena asks me quietly, under her breath, to take her away from there. 'I just want to visit my friends. I will come back, I promise. You can come with me.' She gives me the look. I have been on the street too and understand Haseena well. Sister Cabrini, who used to run the hospice at the time Haseena was brought in, knows that Asha Dan will be stretched to cope with the wiles of the new entrant. 'Haseena is in a pathetic state. I don't know how we can rehabilitate her. She has seen too much too soon. She has been brutalized for too long. Her spirit is scarred. We will have to work out alternative arrangements for her. There is a good chance that she will slip out.'

In my years on the street, I have seen the most abominable expressions of human behaviour. Even the underclass of animal life has more evolved instincts. Haseena's story reeked of the savagery of the rapacious street. When you are cast away from all the accepted parameters of valuable guidance and the street adopts you in its vicious coil, primal urges replace the higher consciousness so comfortably talked about in the comfort of a full belly. It is survival at any cost, and brutality and death are small change!

At about the same time, another young girl was rescued from the clutches of Kamathipura. Tulasa Thapa from Nepal was sold to the brothels of Mumbai by a relative. She ended up in a local hospital with multiple venereal diseases and was finally taken back to Nepal. She made the headlines and a lot was made of the rescue and rehabilitation. (I have narrated her story in greater detail in Chapter 7.)

There were others too, but they are bald names and numbers, occupying territory in a statistician's books. Nothing has changed over the years, and nothing will for a long time. Mumbai's streets are perforated with the carcasses of young, tender lives.

CHAPTER 5

JUHU

The gaudy, blabbing, and remorseful day
Is crept into the bosom of the sea.
                    —William Shakespeare, *King Henry VI Part II*

Mumbai has a chronic shortage of green cover. Land has been plucked out of nowhere and packed with apartment blocks that reach out to the sky. The assault on open spaces continues unabated. There are a few parks but they are sadly inadequate for the burgeoning population. Luckily, the sea is close by and thousands visit the two beaches, one in the south of the city and the other further north.

Both beachfronts boast a heady mix of life. Girgaum Chowpatty in the south is much smaller in spread and carefully patrolled. It is also well-lit and any half chance is seen even in the moonlight. The larger beach in Juhu is a delectable expanse of sand with vast stretches far away from any attention. It is action-packed.

The centre of the beach parades colourful food stalls, there are games for children, and a melange of attractions. Juhu beach is the cheapest fun spot to be in, crowded throughout the week. On weekends the crush on space is suffocating. Privacy is not a culturally friendly notion in India even among the snobbish. While Indians have a soft corner for anything made overseas (sales pitches never forget to mention that the item on the block is imported), they are certainly not enthused by the stiff upper lip. Be a regular at Juhu or in any other crowded area of the city and you will be asked every dark detail of your life. From your salary, address, age, caste, community and father's name to when you last had sex.

It is on weekends that families take a break from the rigours of cloistered living, visit the beach and scatter the air with mirth and laughter. On both sides of the stalls, the beach continues for miles in the shroud of darkness tenanting the flotsam of the city ever ready to flash a razor and anoint it with fresh blood. There is a police presence but it is no deterrent. The cops have a great time. They get massaged and fed gratis, drink openly on the sands, make a pile from everyone who breaks the law and even use a government vehicle with free petrol to drive up and down, ostensibly to keep tabs.

Juhu is an enchanting pie of real estate. It is also well positioned. Colaba is too far south and Mira Road way out in the north. It is the arterial nerve of the hub of the new city that is snaking its way northwards towards Andheri, Goregaon, Borivili and beyond. These are tomorrow's hot spots. There is new money and it will need to find its own expression. In Mumbai, an entire lifetime can be spent commuting and yet not reaching anywhere. So it is imperative that workplaces are not far from residences. An address in Juhu or its vicinity can be a great blessing. It is, in a way, equidistant to the various corners of commerce in the city.

Shaking hands with the sea, Juhu boasts pieces of exquisitely constructed real estate. It is home to the beautiful people, the movers and shakers perennially making waves. It has tastefully designed homes, cafes, art galleries, temples, discos and shops so laden with goodies that you can't help but take a bite. The sea spread is chock-a-block with hotels and specialty restaurants. Several parts of Juhu boast the good life. There is also a significant tourist presence thanks to its central location, its proximity to the sea and the flurry of hotels that provide comfort and choice retakes of sin to the foreign traveller. Like Colaba and several other parts of Mumbai, Juhu also has a wealth of nightlife.

I have spent months on end on Juhu beach. In one incarnation I used it as a bedroom when I was homeless. I was new to the city and couldn't find accommodation to suit my pocket. So the beach was ideal. It was free, less polluted and exciting, which was important. Every night, when I finished up as a reporter in a city newspaper, I would take a fast train and head for the beach. And every night I was rewarded with experiences that kept me on my toes till daybreak. It was far more enriching than taking down a quote pregnant with falsehood and hacking it on an unbreakable Remington typewriter for the unsuspecting reader the next day.

All I needed was a small bag for toiletries and a hardy pair of jeans. If I fell short on sleep, which was often, I found an easy way out. I would buy a balcony ticket for any Hindi film and sleep soundly in air-conditioned comfort for three hours. This invariably became a regular habit, inviting great sympathy from the usher at the cinema who had become my friend and would go out of his way to wipe the seat with his handkerchief. I wasn't sure if that cleaned the seat or dirtied it. The handkerchief clung to his neck, under his collar, for days on end. It had a mucky complexion and always smelt of old sweat. But the gesture smacked of empathy and it was enough to endear him to me. Sometimes, he even allowed me to dip into his packet of popcorn. He told me gravely, one day, that he had also suffered a lot in life!

Later, when I was financially more settled but still clinging hard to old habits, in this case seeking out excitement with a passion, I joined a guitar-wielding group of evangelists. We met at the beach every day and praised the lord. If you are alone, the beach can be dangerous. There were a few murders at that time and it put us on edge for a while, but it was forgotten in no time. Something or the other keeps happening on the beach and old murders get boring. If you are in a group, you attract attention but are safe. We were a mixed crowd of several nationalities and we attracted a lot of attention. Juhu beach was our home. We finished with our various jobs in the day and met at an arranged spot at night. We sang, made barbecues and slept in sleeping bags. We hit the road the next day and spread the message of love. For those cast away on the sands of Juhu, we were certainly worth looking at twice.

Juhu beach also attracts, apart from every other conceivable type of driftwood, what is locally known as the 'struggler'. Hindi cinema draws star-struck young men and women from all over India to Mumbai, where the Hindi film industry is headquartered.

Hindi cinema, like cricket, is a unifying force for a nation living in several time zones and cultures and in extreme poverty. Life hovers on thin ice for millions of Indians. Like a trapeze artiste on a shoestring, the lifeline can give way anytime. It is a void. There are no heroes to emulate. The political system doesn't work. Chances are that it never will, considering the intrinsic inadequacies of the illiterate vote. Nor is there enough food, water, shelter, clothing, education or medical aid for a rapidly growing population.

There is a crushing need to escape the burden of existence, but how? Religion helps. Cricket and Hindi films also open instant escape hatches. So the stars become demigods, much larger than life. They dictate trends, fashions, language and endorse products that the ordinary person would love to acquire. In some parts of India, they have also become deities and are ritually worshipped publicly. Several have become politicians of considerable stature. Their mass appeal is enormous.

The 'struggler' is mesmerized by all this. He wants to be a part of this dream machine. He is from the small towns of India where Hindi cinema gives people a reason to live. He has watched films every waking moment of his life and dresses and talks like his favourite star. Fame and money add to the inducement of belonging to the ferment of potboilers. He believes that he will, given a break, even change the face of world cinema. Little does he realize that, one day, this obsession could also take him to the grave.

I met scores of strugglers on the beach. The film and television industry works largely from the suburbs near Juhu and so the beach is a good place to recharge your failing dreams. One of the strugglers walked around like Steven Spielberg. He cultivated his scruffy look and even recited his Oscar acceptance speech to me several times. 'It will be in English and Punjabi,' he assured me. 'Because I am patriotic.' I almost choked on the hot tea I was drinking.

He then told me the story line of the blockbuster he had in mind. It was set in India, Pakistan and the United States, starring Tom Hanks in the role of a turbaned Sikh. Quite original, but why Tom Hanks, I asked him with a straight face. 'Because he looks innocent,' was his terse reply. He checkmated me with that. He looked worried one day and I asked him what had happened. 'What will I do with all the money I will earn? I couldn't sleep last night. I am worried.' He kept dreaming of the Oscar, the publicity blitz that accompanies it, his space in the spotlight, and all the pecuniary gains waiting to shower on him.

He had run away from a village in Punjab in the north of India as a little boy. His father was the local carpenter and wanted his son to take after him. But one day there was a public screening of a Hindi film starring a hero from his state. He saw the muscular star bash up a gang of hoodlums and nonchalantly jump several hundred feet onto a white horse saddled below. Not a strand of his long mane had left its gelled space and he wore no scratch on his baby pink complexion. The horse also obeyed the hero's shrill whistle with a neigh.

That did it. Impressed and galvanized to action, the lad took the train to Mumbai. He spent a month here and lived off his wits. It got tiring. After a while even scavenging food got difficult, and he went back home to mummy. But the image of the hero jumping on to a horse after a great fight never quite left him. He was smitten for life. He came back to Mumbai after a few years, older and more determined to stay. This time he vowed to return as the star of the silver screen.

He did a series of jobs, visited all the studios, met the stars and took advice from astrologers, who always extracted his last rupee before assuring him that a great future was just round the corner. They gave him rings and amulets to wear and sent him to different temples on different days of the week to appease the deity of the day. One of them even told him that success was assured if he could eat raw dog meat. He did that too. He found a dead dog in a burial ground and cut it up. That didn't help either.

Good looking in a rustic way, he wanted to emulate his childhood hero. But as time passed and some grey sprouted on his scalp, he decided that it made more sense to become a film director. Since the hero had to be youthful looking to blaze the silver screen, he was getting baulked by the passage of time. So he joined the unit of a leading film director. He spent all his money and emotion on this obsession. Hindi cinema consumed him.

We spent evenings on the sands drinking tea. He was in a pathetic state and was always broke. He shared digs with other strugglers, had no change of clothes and very little food. Without intending to insult his fragile ego, I paid his food bills. I told him that it was a loan and he could repay me when he made it big. He grudgingly accepted the kindness prodded by the rumblings in his stomach. Sometimes, when I gathered some nerve, I also told him that Hindi cinema was not such a good career option. He had already wasted so many years and got nowhere in the rough, cruel tumble of a city that has no time for losers. If he wasn't careful, I added politely, it would one day have him for dinner. But he instantly rebuked me. 'You have to dream big. I am talented and handsome. No one understands me because I am ahead of my time. You are also average like the others. Wait and see. I will be on the moon one day. Look at Shah Rukh Khan. He doesn't look good and he can't act. If he can make it, I can.'

He kept rehearsing his Oscar speech till it was almost perfect. When I told him that time was passing him by and he was getting further away from a break in Bollywood, he retorted, 'My stars are not good now. But the astrologer has told me that they are changing from next month's full moon.'

This went on for years. I met him recently. The long wait had got to him. He was defeated, withered and bent. His clothes were worn out and the shoes had holes in them. There was no money even for a cup of tea or even to buy a bus ticket. He had turned surly, took offence at any remark, and stopped talking to me. He was now living on the beach. Late at night, when the stretch was almost deserted, he slept in the scanty undergrowth watched closely by mangy strays wagging their tails gently in sympathy. In the end, hungry and homeless, he quietly left the world he had conjured with so much hope.

I met several others who had run away from the security of their homes in small towns and villages to join the Hindi film industry. Regional cinema is also alive but nothing flickers as brightly as Bollywood and no city is as charmingly seductive as Mumbai. In a few years, the strugglers would get sucked into a life of deprivation. They couldn't return home either. Once you are in the big city for long, it is difficult to get back to the Indian badlands. Your perspective changes and you become another person altogether. Then even recognizing the space you have left behind can get difficult. They had lost out on all counts. The smarter ones got bit roles and did odd jobs or managed to marry well. The majority just faded away in a crumpled heap in some corner of the city.

On moonless nights, several parts of Juhu beach are flooded in darkness. The beach is packed with sex workers and a floating population of customers from all parts of India. Sexual excursions take place openly. Rooms close by are always booked for extended copulation. Everyone understands the space crunch and hotels and restaurants let out time for intimacy. No questions are asked.

'Maalish' or massage is also a big draw. 'Maalishwallas' carry a colourful container of several bottles of oil, clank them together and walk the beach searching for customers. A soiled bed sheet is laid out and different types of massage done. 'Thaliya' is for the feet. Oil is poured on a copper vessel that is rubbed on the feet till it turns black, sucking out the day's tensions from the body. 'Champi' or body massage can be wet or dry depending on your need. There are different oils available at varying prices. An enervating head massage is also offered. For as little as hundred rupees, the whole body can be massaged in aromatic oil on the sands under the stars. It is quite a luxury. There is more if you are interested. Homosexuality is also on call.

'You want massage,' he asks me politely. 'Very good massage.' He is a diminutive fellow with large beady eyes and gelled hair. His hands and feet are huge, so totally disproportionate to the rest of his body. He is clean-shaven with a large mouth. 'I give you best massage,' he continues. 'Where are you from?' The shadows hide many secrets on the beach and suddenly they can spring to life.

I politely refuse and tell him I am Indian, a local chap. 'But you look like from England,' he persists. He then insists that we have a cup of tea and hails a 'chai' boy. 'I will pay,' he assures me. I like his attitude and decide to string him along. 'Here's my card,' he says, thrusting a cheap piece of paper along with his picture and the stamp of a local police station. 'Everyone knows me. I massage the police too. You can ask them about Zanzy. How do you like my name? Do you like my card? Is there a spelling mistake? Is my English good?'

I assure him that it's a great name to have and that it's a beautiful card. 'I change my name every six months. It gets boring. Now I am Zanzy. What should I change my name to? I like Hindi film titles and heroes' names.' I tell him that's really cool and Zanzy is a fine name. I am sure that he will get another great name in a few months. He is happy to hear this and keeps grinning from one large ear to another. He tells me that he likes me and will massage me for free anytime, any place. He also tells me that he never goes back on his word. 'Ask anyone. They all know Zanzy.'

We meet the next day. This time I suggest we have some beer. We get bottles and sit on the beach. 'On Sundays I get a facial and manicure and pedicure done,' he tells me smiling. 'It looks good, no? Don't I have a soft face? Isn't it shining? I massage my friend. He does it free. Actually, I will tell you the truth. Why lie to you? You are my friend. I fuck him and he does my facial.' He flavours the conversation with references to female genitalia. His mother, sisters and girlfriend are included. It is street lingo nourished and tormented by a rush of machismo and a desire to bond with me. He wants me as his buddy and pushes me with the violence of his words to share the tides of the brotherhood of the street. As we talk, the sea and sky are painting gossamer beads.

He then points to an old man sleeping on the beach listening to music from a transistor placed next to his ears. 'He comes everyday looking for boys. Then they do oral.' What about you, I ask. Are you in the game? 'Sure,' he tells me. 'I like you, you want?' He tells me about his clientele. 'I have regulars. They also call me home. Sometimes I massage their wives and get to fuck them both. Women also pick me up on the road. They come in cars and choose the men and take them to some hotel or apartment. They pay me thousand rupees for a good time.'

He tells me about a well-known college nearby. 'Just stand outside. Some aunty will pick you up. Their husbands are sick or they are not married. They will pay you well.' I pretend that I know nothing about all this and that he is lying. 'No, I never lie. Ask anyone. Why don't you stand there tomorrow? You will earn more than me. You are strong and you know English. Aunties will like you. This happens everywhere. Come with me. I will show you.'

Then he pauses for a moment and asks me, 'Is it good to fuck everyday. I am only twenty-four. So it is okay, no? It is the age for fucking. After forty no one fucks, no?' I ask him if he uses condoms. No, he tells me. What about AIDS? There is an HIV counselling and testing centre right on the beach, less than hundred yards from where we are. I ask him to go there. 'I have heard about it, but if I have to die I will die. Who can prevent all this? It is God's will. I pray everyday.'

He then tells me that he is in love. 'Come, meet her,' he says. 'Her name is Preeti. She is a streetwalker. She says that she wants to be my wife and give me children and cook for me. Tell me if you like her. No, no, she said that she would stop going with other men after marriage. What will happen if I fall ill? I am alone in this city. I need someone to look after me, no?'

He strides off. I join him. We walk to a row of autorickshaws on the street. In one of them, parked under a tree, is Preeti. 'Look who I got,' he tells her proudly, flashing his big smile. Zanzy thinks I am a foreigner and wants to introduce me to everybody as his friend. It pushes him up the social ladder. Preeti is thin and short and is dressed in a yellow floral salwar kameez. She is heavily made up and wears red platform shoes. 'Hello,' I say. 'Zanzy talks a lot about you.' She smiles and they hold hands. They talk a bit and she tells him that it is a busy time for her and they will meet later. She says a sweet goodbye to both of us and the rickshaw pushes off. She will drive around and pick up men. Sometimes, the love-making is in the vehicle. That's easy. The cops can't harass a rickshaw on the move. If the customer wants more space and doesn't mind the bribes he has to pay for the comfort, they go to the one-hour rooms nearby.

We walk back for more beer. 'Do you like her?' asks Zanzi. 'Isn't she beautiful?' Yes, I tell him, but you don't have to rush into marriage. Hold on a while. You are still very young. He thinks and says, 'Yes, I agree. Everybody has fucked her. Won't it be strange marrying a girl everyone has fucked? How will I be sure that she won't fuck others behind my back? And then if she gets pregnant from some other man, I will have to give the child my name. Yes, you are right. I must not marry her.' This is not what I had in mind, but there seems no point in explaining anything to Zanzy. He has already moved on. He also keeps talking and manufacturing his own conclusions.

Over the next few months, Zanzy takes me to all the holes in the suburbs around Juhu. We walk through slum colonies that can get claustrophobic even for rodents. But the hovels are thriving with human life. Like birds that have made nests, every type of material, from asbestos and wood to mud, cement and thatching, is used to build homes. Somehow, everyone finds a way to live. The human being is truly indestructible and ingenuous. The flesh trade is also flourishing everywhere: the poorer the quarter, the more virulent its form.

Zanzy tells me about his clients. 'One is a terrorist. He has bullet wounds all over his body. One chap sells arms. Another controls the drug business. The police know everything. We are all "khabris" (informers), me too. The police want to be massaged, but you can't charge them. You have to do it free. I also get them other things when they ask me. You know what I mean. They are very fond of me. Ask anyone about Zanzy.'

One day, from a desolate corner of the beach, Zanzy and I are watching the tide come in. The moon is hiding today and the tide is not ferocious. I watch the water come gently to my feet like an obedient puppy, wander around them, and then withdraw, sucking out the sand from under my toes. Suddenly, my reverie is broken. I am rudely asked to move. I turn around to see a man in a loose white shirt and dark pants. I tell him that the beach is public property and belongs to all of us. He can stay if he wants to, but I am not moving. He stares at me and slowly lifts his shirt. I see a pistol tucked into his pants in the half-light. He continues staring. I get the hint fast. Four other men join him. I look for Zanzy. He has already left. I have no choice, and walk away quickly, expecting a bullet in my back. We are not far from the police station but I know by now that by reporting the matter I will ensure lifelong bother. I catch up with Zanzy in the bright lights of the food stalls and ask him why he turned tail so easily. 'You don't know,' he tells me quietly. 'They are terrorists. I have massaged them. They all have guns.'

Zanzy ran away from home in Madhya Pradesh. 'I am from a good family,' he tells me. 'We are Brahmins. But I wasn't interested in studies and so came to Mumbai and started doing massage. It is very easy. Every day you learn new things.' Several foreigners pick him up and take him to their hotel rooms. He also accompanies them to Goa as their Indian guide and lover. 'I want to make lots of money,' he tells me. 'Lots and lots of money. There is good money in smuggling, no? I can cut my hair, oil it, wear a white shirt, black pant, black shoes and a tie, and put on spectacles. Who will imagine I am a smuggler? They will think I am a professor. I saw it in some film. One of my clients is a smuggler. He said that I could earn a lot of money taking whisky to Gujarat. What do you think? Good, no?'

Zanzy went missing for a long time. I bumped into him months later. His bones were sticking out of his collars and he was coughing violently. His large bulging eyes paraded disease. I gave him the address of a doctor and some money for treatment. I never saw him after that.

He waits patiently for me every day. He knows that I come to the beach in the late evening and he has been watching the road and the stretch of beach touching it for hours. He doesn't want to miss me. Prem Sagar is a short, thin and dark man with bloodshot eyes and a cyst on his forehead. His hair is scanty and his face is hollowed. He smiles with large, broken discoloured teeth. Many decades of a hard life have literally wrenched the flesh off his body. It is raining and his shirt is wet, illuminating his bones. He came from Uttar Pradesh to Mumbai many years ago and scrapes around for a living. His family is still in the village. He earns a little and sends whatever he saves back home for his son's education. 'I believe in hard work,' he tells me with evocative eyes. 'I have to create good karma for my next life.'

But Prem Sagar is not waiting for me for idle chatter or to talk about the afterlife. He has other, more pressing issues to discuss. He is courting a grand obsession. He wants me to connect him with Mallika Sherawat, the actress who smooches, ad libs and drops her clothes without patience. Like millions of other Indians, her voluptuous body fascinates him. 'Please,' he begs me. 'Just one call. I want to hear her voice. I know you are in the film industry and you can do it for me.' I tell him it's difficult, that I am not in the film industry, and why bother to talk to her? See her films and go home and fantasize like the millions.

'I have seen all her films at least ten times each,' he tells me with more passion than a scholar at the Sorbonne poring over the nutrients of ice. 'I have read all the articles on her. I know where she stays and the doctor she visits. But I want to talk to her. I know you can connect me to her.' What will you tell her? You must be decent, no vulgar talk, I insist. 'Of course not. I just want to hear her voice and tell her that she is a great actress and that I have seen her films several times. I promise no vulgar talk. I just want to hear her voice, that's all.'

I tell him that the time is not right and that she is on an overseas shoot. He looks disappointed and then says fine, next time. This happens every day. I can't shrug him off.

For the migrants to the city the obsession with Hindi cinema is aggressive. All the Hindi films are seen and discussed several times. Yesterday's hero Jeetendra walks on the beach in a tight black T-shirt and shorts at a furious clip late in the evening. Whenever they see him they stare. Some follow him and try to talk to him but Jeetendra puts his head down and ups the pace. Well past his sixties and wafer trim, he is faster than the boys who follow him. All the boys have their ears pierced, are draped in accessories, and have cut their jeans with blades near the thighs and knees after Shahrukh Khan in some film. Hairstyles, walking styles and drawls are all copied from some actor or the other. I can't explain it or understand it. Neither can I tell them that their lives should make more sense. They are dead to reason.

Word has, by now, strangely, got around that I am from the industry and can shape their dreams. They all come, one by one, and touch my feet every evening. It is embarrassing. I tell them to go back home, that I have no connection whatsoever with Hindi cinema, that this is a wasted dream, that time is precious. It will make more sense thrusting their youth on other things. But my words don't reach them. I also know that they won't return home. There is nothing to go back to.

Mumbai dazzles. It is a heroin fix. Every day unfolds with hope and beckons hundreds of thousands of migrants to its hollows. Once they are plugged to the energy of the city, all sanity is vacuumed. Their only hope now is in slum development schemes, vote bank politics, a life of crime or even something as bizarre as being hit or run over by a rich man's car. If they survive the accident, there will be good money paid for their silence. If they don't, the next of kin have a windfall.

'I see you every night here. What do you do? What if I take a knife and thrust it into you? What will you do?' I am having tea in a shack on the beach near the Marriott Hotel. He joins me, grabs a cup of tea, sits next to me and keeps staring at me. 'You are a foreigner?' I tell him that I am Indian and have nothing on me barring a hundred rupees. Anyone can take it without showing me a knife. I ask him if he wants it. He is impressed. 'Only hundred rupees? I have five hundred rupees.' He digs it out of his pocket to show me. Good for you, I say.

'I am Mashaal. Can you give me a job? I have come from Bihar.' Mashaal is slim and well dressed and has fashionable sunglasses peeking out of his shirt pocket. He also talks good English. But his young teeth are broken and stained and his eyes are lost in some other era. I can tell that he is a regular hashish smoker. The signs are obvious. They all smoke on the beach. 'I studied till tenth standard. I know computers also. Give me a job.' He says he is twenty-two and married with a daughter. He is a tourist guide. 'Ask for anything. I will get it for you. You want good girls, college girls, aunties, drugs, actresses, what you want?' He keeps staring at me with lost eyes. His body language is not friendly and I don't want trouble. Not today, I tell him, and walk away. But I can see him following me from the corner of my eye.

No open space in Mumbai is far from a sex worker. There are scores of them on Juhu beach, well protected by the law. If you are caught with your girlfriend, the police will pounce on you. But if you get intimate with a sex worker, they will encourage the dalliance.

I walk a few hundred yards and meet Rekha. She holds my hand and says gleefully, 'Come, let's enjoy. You can pay later. I see you everyday.' She is short, filled out with a vengeance, resembles an

Indian temple carving, and is very charming in a green saree. She also knows her lines. 'You look nice and decent, not like other men.' She tells me the rates and all that she can do, almost as fast as a waiter in an Udipi restaurant reciting the menu. She also tells me that if I am not comfortable here we can go wherever I want to take her. 'I can drink, take hashish, do French, back sex, front sex, hand job, whatever you want. My family is in Kolkata. My daughter is studying. Can you help? I need money.'

In the weeks to follow I meet up with Rekha several times and get to know her. After her work, she takes me to all-night bars not too far away from the beach and we drink to her health. She is a beautiful woman: charming, articulate, loving, kind, polite and distractingly well-stacked. On our second 'date', she insists on paying the bill because she has made a lot of money that night. It was a holiday and she had a windfall. Her only crime is that she was born poor. The brutality of her circumstances gets me at the core but I am helpless. Apart from giving her some money and telling her to insist on condoms, I can't do anything else.

He knows more about Juhu beach than any other person. His hair and thick sideburns, barring a growing bald patch on the crown, are dyed black and his dark, clean-shaven face is proud and chiselled. His smile is an I-know-it-all smirk and he walks ramrod stiff, bent slightly back from the torso as though he is leading the Republic Day parade. His sartorial sense is old-world: bell-bottoms, leather slippers and a long, loose full-sleeved shirt. The beach is his home and his office. Anthony Bhai is in charge of all the little 'dhandas' that operate on a tiny stetch of sand. Different areas of the beach are controlled by different people. Like the stray dogs who have sharply defined territories, one doesn't step into the other's domain. They are also under the jurisdiction of different police stations. So, like the monsoon which chooses which stretch of the city to rain on, the raids on the beach are also selective.

The 'dhandhas' are not injurious to health. They include a few games, children's rides and coconut and 'bhel' stalls. Anthony Bhai employs many people and he just hangs around, smoking cigarette after cigarette, overseeing the work. The municipality conducts raids sometimes and the police are always on hand. But Anthony Bhai does the balancing act well. He knows how to talk and whom to pay, and still manage a good income.

I have been watching him for months and we haven't exchanged a word, but one day, for some unfathomable reason, he comes over and starts talking. Once he starts, he won't stop even if the city is burning. He also loves repeating his story countless times. He tells me about his life. About his family, his work, the money he makes, the payments to staff and various government agencies and his habits like swimming in the sea in the hot summer months. 'I have written the story of my life in a book but it got washed away in the monsoon. I could have given that to you. I believe you are a writer. You could have used it. It is a bestseller. You can even make a film on it.' Yes, he wants to be written about and, for a change, I am not in camouflage.

He tells me about his lifestyle in great detail. He sleeps before the clock strikes midnight on a thin cloth spread on the beach and wakes up at five every morning, walks to the marketplace across the road for his ablutions and a cup of tea. It doesn't matter which time of the year it is. 'I haven't had formal education but I have learnt a lot on my own,' he tells me. 'I read the papers and sometimes watch television.' He talks about the news channels, how they get advertising, about Animal Planet and National Geographic. There is a lot of wisdom in his words. As I get to know him over the next few months, I realize that, yes, Anthony Bhai is a master strategist at survival. He will do well anywhere. Starvation is not in his horoscope. His DNA is wired for success even without Deepak Chopra.

'I don't do any "faltu" talk. There is no one to talk to here anyway. They are all illiterate. "Kala akshar bhains barabar." I do

103

my job, sleep, wake up early and, sometimes, take a nap in the hot summer months. The authorities have asked me to vacate but I have explained to them that I am not building a bungalow here. I don't own any part of the beach and it is not my ambition either. Sleeping here is not comfortable. It is just convenience. They have understood me now.'

We have chai and as I feed the strays, he continues, 'It is all a money game. What isn't? You tell me. You pay and you get things done. It starts at the top and goes right down to the bottom. Even a cup of tea costs money. You sit here everyday. You pay to come here and go back, even if it is bus fare, and you pay for your chai. So you are paying just to watch the sea. Am I right or wrong? Even watching the sea is not free, even breathing clean air is not free.' I tell him that he is absolutely right and he likes the answer. Now there is no containing him.

Anthony Bhai was born a Muslim but a Hindu saint prophesied it all and he was brought up by Christians. I love Anthony Bhai's story. He has no time for religion; work is his only God. Barring his cigarettes and his high-protein non-vegetarian diet, he has no other interest. I ask him if he visits the women on the beach. 'No way. I have nothing to do with them, no interest at all. My work is my worship. It is their livelihood. Let them do what they have to do. We all fill our stomachs in different ways. It is their way. God bless them.'

He shows me wads of notes in his wallet bulging out of his back pocket. He has a bank account, pays his staff everyday and has saved enough for a decent living. What if he is robbed? 'No one dare touch my wallet. He will be caught in no time. They won't even dream of it.' Why do you carry so much money always? 'Lots of payments have to be made to many people,' he says with his usual smirk.

While we chat, a cop in a sea-blue safari suit lands up. He greets us and joins the conversation. He is Anthony Bhai's friend.

He tells me that he will be retiring soon after more than three decades in the force. I look at him hard. The close-cropped hair and moustache are dyed black, his shoes are polished and there is, surprisingly, no paunch. He looks very trim for a man in his late fifties. He also wears a saint's demeanour and has large, innocent eyes. He also quotes the Gita and the Vedas. I look harder at him. Is he a Mumbai cop??

Weeks later, terrorists from Pakistan create mayhem by taking over the Taj Mahal Palace Hotel and shooting at will. A handful of trained teenagers from across the border make the Mumbai police look like awkward schoolgirls at their first prom night. Senior officers are audaciously shot dead and policemen at the Chhatrapati Shivaji train terminus are unable to even load their rifles. They couldn't even have shot coloured balloons at the shooting gallery run by Anthony Bhai on the beach. The cops are the laughing stock of an embarrassed political establishment. The whole world watches on television how inadequately trained and equipped they are. The entire nation of over a billion people stands up and choruses that the cops are nothing more than a useless, unfit, corrupt and scandalous bunch of gravediggers. India has been saying this for decades. Now, thanks to the terrorists, some changes in the force may happen.

I am on the beach again having my chai and feeding the dogs when the old cop lands up. He looks dapper in a smart, well-fitting police uniform. He has a pistol, too, which looks menacing in its holster. You guys couldn't fight teenagers, I chide him. What are you doing with a pistol now after all the carnage is over? 'Oh no,' he exclaims. 'You don't know the truth. Do you know what is happening in the force, do you know what a cop's life is like? I can't talk now. Let me retire and I will tell you the whole story. I agree with whatever you and the others say but please listen to our side of the story too. Everyone thinks that we are a bunch of corrupt, useless fellows. There are good reasons for all this.' Then he pauses, thinks, and adds, 'Do you know that even this uniform I have bought with my own money. The uniform they gave me was terrible. So I stitched my own. I wanted some pride while wearing it. Also, let me tell you that every cop is not the same, every finger is different.'

I ask him about the pistol. 'They have given me this for a few weeks. Then they will take it away. We don't need firearms for regular bandobast. Also, this pistol can only shoot accurately for a few yards. It loses its accuracy after that.' Have you guys been training regularly? 'Please wait, let me retire,' he assures me. 'I will tell you the whole story. I can't say anything now. You have no idea of the pulls and pressures on us.' Close by two teenagers are piling on each other. They have probably hit the beach after telling their parents that they have gone for tuitions. The cop sees them, too. They are an ideal target for a bribe. Threaten to report the matter to their folks and they will give you all their change, their jewellery and their mobile phones. I watch the moment. But, this time, the cop isn't interested. Moral policing has no takers after the terrorist attack.

But there is such a thing as bogus policing. In fact, the new devil on the beach is the bogus cop. He has realized that policing is a lucrative business and has spread out to all corners of the city. The beach, of course, is a venue he simply cannot afford to miss.

The imposter dresses up as a cop. When he is not in police uniform, he is in mufti. Heavy built, with a short haircut and moustache, a white full-sleeved shirt flowing silkily over his paunch, he pounces on the unwary. In the faint light of a clouded moon, when you are mooching away, the finer details are often overlooked, especially if it is the strong arm of the law bearing down on you. The first thoughts are to confess, pay whatever you can and hurriedly escape the dragnet. More laws have been made than anyone can remember and so almost everyone is breaking some law or the other.

No one wants to go the police station and so the bogus cop has a field day. A colleague of mine on an evening stroll was 'caught' by a bogus cop. Since he wasn't breaking any law, he stood his ground and asked the cop for his identity card. When the imposter realized that he had caught a media person, he fled. There was a scuffle before that. My colleague pinned him down and tore his shirt but the imposter managed to wriggle away. I was a few hundred feet away having chai and so missed out on the action. But youngsters necking away and those propositioning sex workers are in the net.

The bogus cops even have a training school where their cop mannerisms are chiselled. The real cops have put up warnings everywhere, and now they are not only looking for robbers but also for cops!

As I walk on the beach, the dogs clamour for more biscuits. Every month new puppies are dumped on the beach by those who don't know what to do with their pet's litter. There is also a hungry bitch with bloated teats and the ravenous appetite of a new mother. It is easy to see that motherhood pleases her. She feasts on whatever is thrown at her and then gets down to the joy of suckling her babies. Like a lot of human beings, she has also skipped the family planning net.

One of the regulars, brown, frail and toothless, is a 'widower'. He has to munch the biscuits carefully, after a lot of deliberation, with his side molars. He looks at the biscuit, examines it from all sides and feigns disinterest until another dog eyes it keenly. That galvanizes his appetite. He has had a long and steady relationship and several puppies with a beautiful brown bitch. One day, she just stopped eating, was reduced to skin and bones, and died. He looked hard at her lifeless body for a few minutes and walked away. I wonder what he was thinking; his partner won't be around anymore for love and frolic, would he miss her? Does he know about death, would he mourn, would he worry about his own mortality, would he find another lover easily?

I call him Horny Atma. He has a human soul with the dog's instincts in place. He is tactile and wants to be fed and cuddled and loves being spoken to in English. He will smile at your words and wag his bushy little tail. He loves it. He goes to everyone on the beach and they all talk to him and he is happy. You can also talk to him in any dialect. If he is not a linguist, he just loves the sound of human words. Horny Atma comes alive in the rutting season in the cool winter months. He is not top dog anymore and has to cower in submission when the younger studs with full teeth snarl at him. But he still retains the charm and cunning to promise a mate healthy offspring. Even if he doesn't get the best bitch, he manages to sell a straggler sweet little lies. Despite his slowly depleting hormone charge, he remains the king of con.

'Good morning, sar,' says a voice from behind me. I turn around and see Mashaal, the tourist guide and procurer from Bihar whom I haven't seen for ages. 'Where have you been?' I ask. He remains silent and I notice a little snot-nosed boy trying to stop his torn shorts from falling off his genitals. Who is this, I ask. 'My son, sar.' Congratulations, but it may be a good idea to stop at one child, I tell him. Earn a livelihood before you bring more kids into the world. Use condoms or go to a government hospital and they will do 'nasbandi' and even pay you for it. There is silence. 'I have one more child, sar, a daughter.' One more child, but you don't have money for breakfast! 'What can I do, sar? It is God's will.' Well, then, the gods must be crazy.

It is all getting too heavy and I decide to visit the loo, which once hosted a condom-vending machine on the outside wall. The condoms and the coins inserted got stuck and the machine rusted and was finally removed. The urinal is multipurpose and hazardous. I have to step over sleeping dogs and human beings, other men keen on 'sizing' me up, and inhale large doses of urea. It is much easier to pee in the sea!

CHAPTER 6

SAUNDATTI

*Nothing discernible to the eye of the spirit is more brilliant or obscure
than man; nothing is more formidable, complex, mysterious, and
infinite. There is a prospect greater than the sea, and it is the sky,
there is a prospect greater than the sky, and it is the human soul.*
— Victor Hugo, *Les Miserables*

I met Anagha at Saundatti.

We had been on the road for over a day and most of the
night. The powerful and spacious Mahindra Armada pushed
all cylinders through the hustle of Mumbai city traffic and then
hacked a path on the long and weary national highway into
Karnataka. The highways, like the rest of India, are never empty.
Large, colourfully-painted lorries dot them like bloated carcasses.
Death is always round the corner. Yet, drivers step on the pedal
savagely to swallow the miles in a hurry. This is strange in a land
well known for its disrespect for punctuality, and forever basking
in lazy contemplation. Cosmic time presides over most of India.
Even in the richer urban centres driven by profit, habitual late-

coming is pardoned. It is not an offence. India lumbers along. It is never in a hurry. So this quest for speed is difficult to fathom. But India is also a land rich in contradictions,

It is early morning when we arrive at Saundatti, a dot on the map that seems to have spilled out of Maharashtra and landed first bounce into Karnataka next door like a wrongly hit return of serve. We have made it in time for the first full moon in January and for the dedication ceremony of thousands of young girls to the Goddess Yellamma as Devadasis. (A Devadasi is a servant of god. In a religious tradition, girls are 'married' and dedicated to a deity. Historically, these women learned and practised Indian artistic traditions and enjoyed a high social status.)

Light rain tattoos the Armada's bonnet and churns the soft earth under its unrelenting tyres into slush. The landscape is now bathed in the joyous colours of festivity. Hundreds of thousands of families from Maharashtra, Karnataka, Goa and Andhra Pradesh, all neighbouring states, have made the long journey to Saundatti on foot, cycles, buses, lorries, tempos and rickshaws. 'Udehyo Udheyo Yellamma Udheyo' (Rise up to the mother), scream the believers.

The dedication ceremony happens several times a year. But the full moon in January is a special day. It is auspicious. It occurs exactly one month before the harvest. Devadasis carry water pots on their heads as symbols of the Mother Goddess's power to seduce the male sky god. In Hinduism, female energy is Shakti, and far more sensuous than that of the male. Saundatti, on such a day, is filled with so much energy. It quivers in a cocktail of male, female, eunuch and celibate power.

Stalls of all kinds, eerie ceremonies, extravagant displays of inebriation, dances, songs and talking in tongues knock the stuffing out of reason as ritual, superstition and blind belief superimpose their presence on the moment. The sobriety of a tiny, landlocked, nondescript piece of land in south-central India, which lies dead and arid in the summer, inhospitable even to a

shy blade of grass, and is swollen with water in the rain, is now
steamrolled into cathartic mode. Energy, emancipation, liberation
and thanksgiving coalesce into a mailed fist of such immense
clout that the dedication ceremony of child brides, illegal in the
eyes of the law and beyond the ambit of all reason, acquires new
meaning. 'Udheyo Udheyo Yellamma Udheyo' screams the wind,
the rain, the wet earth and the open sky. The grand opera includes
hundreds of thousands of lusty throats.

It is here that I meet Anagha again. The last time we met she
was a talkative sex worker in one of the cages of Kamathipura in
Mumbai. She was excellent copy, eager to shout from the rooftops
all eighteen years of her life. She was gaudily made up and joked
and laughed a lot. She was also in a hurry to condemn, with choice
expletives, the men who didn't want her. Even the ones who fancied
her were not spared. She could also don the role of the elegant
courtesan when she wanted to, which was most of the time.

But at Saundatti Anagha is different. She is quiet and subdued.
It is as though she has been fitted with another incarnation. Her
head bowed, eyes cast down, Anagha walks in step with a group
of women in the throes of reverence. On her head, carefully held
by both hands, is a three-foot green-and-gold statue of Goddess
Yellamma, not good-looking by any yardstick but not as fearsome
either as some other Indian goddesses. 'Udheyo Yellamma Udheyo',
Anagha chants from deep within the recesses of her throat.

Flourescent turmeric drenches her matted dreadlocks and
long leaves of neem tied around her slim waist anaesthetize her
body from sin. A colourful saree coiled around her like a mating
serpent gingerly holds her young, shapely breasts. The ceremony
takes hours. The long line of women, in the irrational holds of
devotion, moves slowly. The women are in a trance. Some seemed
possessed by spirits and dance like dervishes to an unseen drum
beat, others talk in tongues that are unintelligible. They walk
down several steps to a large pond and enter the cool waters. And

then, purified, emerge like mermaids with neem leaves and cloth clutching their cleansed bodies in a wet hug. Thousands watch, hijras dance and sing.

I join the clamour, and wait for Anagha to emerge from the excesses of the moment.

'I was brought here as a child,' she tells me on the last day, when the vast crowds are readying for the long journey home. She will return to Mumbai in a red-and-yellow government bus and once again take her position as the jewel of her tiny brothel. 'I was dedicated to Goddess Yellamma as a Devadasi. It is my duty and privilege to serve any man. I have divine sanction. I come here every year to reaffirm my faith.'

She believes every word. The red and white beads around her neck speak of her allegiance and bondage. She will stand enticingly at the entrance of her tiny cage in Kamathipura, reinforced in the belief that the satiation of male desire is the sole reason for her existence on Mother Earth. It will make her a better, more accommodating sex worker. She will not ever question the strange forces of circumstances that have condemned her to a life of sexual servitude.

The dedication ceremonies are simple and swift. The ones I witness take place on a hillock. The rain comes down in clumsy drops, and large pregnant clouds watch eagerly. The parents bring the child brides to the temple and face the black-faced stone idol. If the child has discoloured skin or gums, it is considered a good omen from Yellamma. When she grows up, a roll of dreadlock, sometimes hidden under the rest of her hair, will mark her out as a Devadasi.

It is their first 'marriage' and the children are decked in clothes and ornaments. The priest, also drunk by the occasion and its attendant privileges, recites a few mantras, ties the red and white beads around the children's necks and the 'marriages' are complete. There is no prolonged chanting like in other Hindu marriages.

113

I try to get the priest to talk but he is either too frightened to open his mouth or a bit too juiced up. He just stares at me and mutters something unintelligible. The children are then taken home. In all probability, they will be auctioned to the highest bidders, who will keep them till they are well-worn. After that, the young girls will hit the flesh markets of the big cities ready to fulfil their destinies as the handmaidens of the Goddess Yellamma.

There are many theories to explain the origins of the Devadasi system. The most plausible is the one that points to the conspiracy of the upper classes to strengthen their hold on the dispossessed. It is believed that the priestly and warrior classes, fearing reprisals from the tillers of the land, who also outnumbered them considerably, invented a method to perpetuate their economic and sexual hold on the peasantry. India is still hobbled by caste. Hundreds of years ago, it was much worse. The upper classes were born to privilege. They could choose the women of their choice from the landless poor and get away with it without protest. When they sensed that dissent was inevitable, a system of concubines with religious sanction was manufactured. India has countless gods and goddesses for every occasion and there is blind faith. So, a goddess was conjured out of thin air and the peace maintained. Both sides seemed happy with the arrangement. Times changed and it all degenerated into organized prostitution.

But the root cause is the acute poverty that still suffocates most of India. A girl child has always been considered a burden and dedicating her to a goddess was, and still is, the easiest way to escape all responsibility of raising the money needed to buy her a husband. Yellamma's followers are poor, low-caste bonded farm labourers who are in debt for generations. But once their daughters are dedicated to the goddess and become Devadasis, she does not require a dowry. Marriage to Yellamma also ritually converts a daughter into a groom and a son. So poor parents without sons dedicate their last daughter to the goddess as a pension scheme for their old age. For if the daughter becomes a Devadasi, she will have no in-laws or another home to belong to. She will be there, like a son, for the final rites of her parents.

Hundreds of years ago, the Devadasis lived in temples as chaste virgins meant for the gods. In medieval India they were the most cultured and educated women. They learnt to read and write and owned property. They were acclaimed for their skills in dance, music and love-making. There are several theories about them shrouded in discrepancies. A lot depends on the interpretation.

Legend has it that Goddess Renuka, the wife of the sage Jamadagni, was so chaste that she could carry water in a vessel made of fresh clay. One day when she went to the river for her ablutions, she saw a handsome man and was struck with a deep longing for him. All of a sudden, the clay pot burst and Jamadagni, who was in samadhi, realized that his wife had been unfaithful in her thoughts. Enraged, he asked one of his sons to behead Renuka. One of them, Parsuram, beheaded his mother. Pleased with his son, Jamadagni granted him a wish. Parsuram asked for his mother's life. At that moment, Yellamma, a Harijan or low-caste woman, walked by. Her head was placed on Renuka's corpse and she rose, alive now, as Renuka Yellamma. Parsuram's three brothers who refused to obey their father were cursed into becoming eunuchs. This probably explains the huge turnout of hijras at the Yellamma festival.

The Karnataka Prevention of Dedication Act came into force in January 1984. All dedications of child brides to Goddess Yellamma have been officially banned. The police have increased their watch but they are helpless. 'If we see something we can stop it,' one of them told me at Saundatti. 'But what do we do if we don't see anything? They can do the ceremony anywhere, even at home. They want to do it. No one is forcing them to do it. We are forcing them to stop. The law is helpless against the will of the people.'

A slew of rehabilitation measures have been taken by the government and NGOs. Rehabilitation and vocational training centres have been set up, financial assistance arranged for marriages, schools for children of Devadasis established, manufacturing centres for their produce launched, and several campaigns initiated against the Devadasi system. But it still continues in muted form.

I return to Mumbai and meet with those who know about Yellamma and the dedications and have been closely following it for years. Devidas Manohare, a thin, soft-spoken man in his forties, has been working with sex workers as a professional social worker for years. He has an encyclopaedic knowledge of the undercurrents of India's socioeconomic burps. 'As long as there is poverty and illiteracy, the Devadasi system will flourish,' he tells me. 'No law can change anything.' Radha Murali, in her nineties, dedicated to the goddess at the age of seven, believes that the time has come for the Devadasi system to end. 'What I have suffered, nobody else should,' she says emphatically.

But the real world is unreal. 'Today more than half the Devadasis are sex workers. When they grow old they become beggars. The temple rituals have decreased over the years but the dedications have increased,' says Sadhna Zadbuke, a social scientist. The consequences are reinforced by Dr Jeanette Rodrigues, who has been testing the Devadasis in Pune for HIV. 'More than half of them are HIV-positive,' she says. Dr Shilpa Merchant of the Population Services International (PSI), an NGO in Mumbai, agrees. 'The Devadasis are definitely more prone to HIV as they are dedicated as children. Their sexual exposure starts very early.'

I met Anagha several times after this. The brothel she belongs to had been included in the government's AIDS intervention campaigns. The girls were given free condoms every day and instructed on their use. The initiative and its spin-offs were carefully monitored. Free medicines were provided and the neighbourhood was disinfected.

Despite the odds stacked against her, Anagha carried the exuberance of youth. She laughed, played hopscotch with the others on the tiny strip of earth outside the brothel and never, even once, shed a tear for the fate that had consumed her in such a dreadful spell. She told me that she would go again next year to pay obeisance to the Goddess Yellamma on that patch of land on a hillock in faraway Saundatti. 'You will also come, no?' she asked me with the enthusiasm of a child planning a picnic. 'Please come. I will feel happy.' In a dark corner of the brothel the statue of Yellamma, encased in green and gold, looked on seemingly pleased with what she had just heard.

Not so long ago, on the nippy full moon day of Randi Hunnime, an unusual ceremony was observed in the villages of Belgaum in north Karnataka. Rejecting an age-old custom of breaking bangles to observe a one-month period of 'widowhood' with Goddess Yellamma prior to the January full-moon festival, groups of Devadasis performed a reverse ceremony. They wore bangles and took an oath rejecting the demeaning status of Devadasis.

Could this be the first step in the long journey of freedom for the handmaidens of Goddess Yellamma?

CHAPTER 7

GOA AND KATHMANDU

Pick yourself up, dust yourself down, and start all over again.
—Fred Astaire and Ginger Roberts

Goa is a waltz away from Mumbai. Buses, trains, boats, cabs and airplanes take you there whenever you want to, which, for a lot of people, is quite often. It is the backpacker's dream, the ideal weekend getaway, and the ultimate escape. You can hit the hush of the beaches, get lost in the cackle of the marketplace, wander the thick jungles or visit old temples and churches. If this isn't enough, there are sultry taverns, offering food and drink the gods would cherish. Wild full moon parties, nude sun worshippers, flea markets and the simple joy of living unnoticed add to the idyll.

This tiny slice of land on the west coast of India is charged with a timeless and laidback air. Local buses rattle along, cabbies are always listening to music and everyone's waiting to tell the story of their lives over large gulps of feni. It doesn't matter if they have done it an hour ago, and it doesn't bother them if they don't know you too well either. When they are through with this, they play football. Even Panaji, the capital, sleeps in the afternoon. Before that, it just ambles along. After that, it is too late for strenuous exertion.

When Osho was in bloom in the 1970s and 1980s, large numbers of his colourful disciples made for Goa from his Pune commune not too far away. They lived on isolated beaches in rented huts away from the rat race, smoked, drank and made love in their eagerness for super consciousness. The hippies had found Goa even before that. Tired of having to make ends meet in monotonous persuasions, people from all over the world flocked to Goa. Some passed through as tourists, others just thought that it was too much of a bother going back home after Goa happened to them, and simply settled down. They integrated well into the local community and, without quite intending to, kickstarted the tourist boom. The therapeutic call of lethargy is now garbed in commerce under the epaulet of the hospitality industry. 'Susegad', the Goan word for the easy life, and its attendant privileges have spawned big business. In many ways, the liberal air that descended on Goa was not a new import. It was only an extension of the native soul.

Verla-Parra in Bardez in north Goa is a combine of 'vaddos' (hamlets) luxuriating in high-quality 'susegad'. Parra, as the locals know it, subscribes to this overwhelming enchantment with nothingness with an elaborate, unhurried yawn. Under a scorching summer sun, all life seems to have escaped from even the dust. The 'vaddos' have quaint, brightly painted bungalows with manicured gardens, a dry, lonely tar road that beckons the rest of the world without any clamour, and a peace that would embarrass the dead.

India has had twenty-four years of HIV/AIDS. This is a serious concern for a nation of over a billion people. Acknowledging the possible devastation that HIV could cause, the intervention campaigns have been strident. Today, India is well seized of the situation. It has the nemesis cornered and systems are in place to combat the most demonic strains of the virus.

But the long story of HIV/AIDS in India began, at some level, in the idle dust of Verla-Parra.

Dominic Marcus D'Souza, a simple, carefree, happy young man from this little-known 'vaddo' died of AIDS in 1992. It was just another death in statistical terms but it opened a cauldron of worms. It was Dominic's death that led to amendment in legislation, allowed the popular voice to be heard and readied India with knowledge and compassion to face the onslaught of a little-known killer disease that would soon swallow large chunks of the human race.

I used to hang around the beaches of Goa those days and gaze longingly at the hot sun and the moods of the sea. I would swim, fish, get massaged (a touch of shiatsu sometimes), binge on 'sorpotel' and feni, kick the ball viciously in local soccer games, ride on rickety buses and allow myself to be swallowed by the smells and sounds of the marketplace. At night, when little stars invaded the sky, I would play chess with American marines wounded in Vietnam now relaxing on solitary stretches of beach. They skinny-dipped, cooked the fish they caught underwater with bare hands and spent time smoking, reading, choosing girlfriends from the colourful stream of backpackers, and watched the changing colours of the setting sun until it blanked out from view. They were tough and hardened, and had survived the swamps to tell their tale. Goa was so different from Vietnam and they were in no hurry to leave.

I would listen to the blues and their stories and pretend that I had also been holed up in a prisoner-of-war camp in some damp jungle and tortured mercilessly. I wore their old fatigues and even copied their drawl. Sometimes, I would limp like them and look at scratches on my arms and imagine that they were bullet or shrapnel wounds. I felt that I was one of them. It seemed the thing to do on Vagator beach when you were idling away the fantasies of youth. I had read all the books and seen all the films on war. The GI and his exploits were simply unforgettable.

The wind howled and knew that I was lying, that it was all pretence, but never, not even once, did it whistle on me. When I wasn't playing GI, I joined the full moon parties at Anjuna beach and watched the moon dive into the sea in a perfect loop. The early morning sun would then scratch the horizon awake, gently caressing the tall coconut palms and the boulders strewn around them. Spent, stoned bodies would then be delivered from the sanctuary of their delirium.

The full moon parties caught hold of everyone's minds with bare hands and just wrenched them out of their sockets. The music and dancing continued non-stop, sometimes for days on end, and you did what you wanted to. Your mind tripped, phantoms escaped and devils danced on cabbage leaves. There were sun worshippers, yogis, Aikido masters, ballet dancers, Israeli soldiers, Iranian refugees, nudists, painters, bestselling authors, champion board sailors, religious fundamentalists, wheatgrass-chomping herbalists, Hollywood stars, astronomers, power lifters, gypsies, seers, Wall Street analysts, oncologists, international spies, Kenyan marathoners, beautiful babes and gawking Indians, among others.

Anjuna beach attracted the world's quirkiest. This tiny stretch of sand, with boulders, coconut trees and a sprinkling of huts, a hillock away from Baga and Calangute and within a screech of sanity, made a hole in your skull and purged a lifetime of accumulated crap. Before you knew it, that drained, little hole bubbled with a new Utopia.

But now it was time to get into action mode, to scout for information on Dominic D'Souza and the strange disease that killed him which, at that time, had just entered India as an unwelcome guest. Little did I know then that this unfriendly visitor would also overstay.

Verla-Parra does everything it can to avoid the limelight. But when Dominic died, the world lifted its shutters and peered in. Its favourite son had left his body in Mumbai's Breach Candy hospital. He had died of AIDS-related complications, from a disease that had entered India's doors insidiously. Before his death, Dominic was arrested for being HIV-positive like a petty criminal, incarcerated in a rundown TB sanatorium and ostracized by society, the medical profession and the law. It wasn't until impassioned pleas for justice rocked Goa and the limelight sought Verla-Parra, that existing legal and attitudinal responses towards HIV/AIDS were touched with some compassion.

When Dominic tested HIV-positive, not much was known about AIDS in India. Disaster makes news and AIDS made a lot of noise. The reports were dramatic and sketchy. Some said that it was a disease that came from monkeys; others said that foreigners transferred it. The black man, then the white man, the homosexual and, finally, the sex worker were targeted as conduits of virus transmission. A theory that the virus was made in a laboratory and was a tool in biological warfare was also bandied about.

There were no medicines and you were told that if you got the HIV, you would not only die soon but also pass it on while you were alive to several people who could, in turn, infect others. It was a sexual disease without a cure. Nostradamus had mentioned this hundreds of years ago. Now the world would finally come to an end. The moralists and those who were sexually challenged had a field day. The party boys and girls would now be burnt by a Saturday night fever that would roast them in hell, they said in self-righteous joy.

The death of Dominic D'Souza started the process of ending this type of misinformation. In a strange way, he had to die for India to live.

It all began without warning. On the morning of 14 February 1989, a local policeman knocked on Dominic's door with a request that he report to the Mapusa police station without delay. Assuming that a friend was in trouble, Dominic rushed across after a hurried breakfast. From the police station he was taken to a local hospital. Two constables accompanied him. While he was medically examined, the guard was increased. Now there were six policemen, some with rifles, others with lathis. Dominic just couldn't figure out what was happening. It was only later when a register titled AIDS was brought in and Dominic's name entered, that he realized the gravity of the call. He was then whisked away by armed guard to a former TB sanatorium. There he was subjected to forced isolation under the Goa Public Health Act. The whole operation was doused in speed and secrecy. Despite repeated requests, Dominic was prevented from contacting his old mother or close friends.

Since HIV/AIDS was unheard of until then, no one knew what to do. Even its mode of transmission was unclear. The doctors who came everyday to check Dominic stood outside the room, masked their faces like astronauts and asked questions. They were scared; if the virus passed on so easily, wouldn't they get infected too? They were unsure of the modalities of treatment. There was no precedent and so no management protocols, and they didn't want to take chances. Along with his food, he was given Liv-52 and B-complex tablets to boost his immune system. That was the only palliative the medical community could think of.

A month passed and the Goa state government and the state Directorate of Health Services (DHS) were still undecided about amending the Public Health Act, which made isolation mandatory for those who tested HIV-positive. There was genuine paralysis. All government policies were frozen. If the HIV was an import, then tourism, which propped Goa, would also be badly hit. What would they do with the thousands of foreigners already there? There would be an economic collapse. Meanwhile, Dominic continued to languish in solitary like a hardcore criminal waiting for the death sentence. And his failing health continued to deteriorate.

In a bid to free Dominic, his friends frenetically contacted an NGO in Mumbai. Press conferences, demonstrations, protest marches, media coverage and legal intervention finally pressured the government into releasing him after sixty-four long days. And a little over three years after his arrest, Dominic took his last breath.

'I knew what AIDS was,' wrote Dominic a few months before his death in *Wise Before Their Time*, a confessional compilation by Positive People, a project that was launched to offer care and hope to those who tested HIV-positive. 'But I never really educated myself. I knew how it is transmitted, but I never practised safe sex. I had this feeling that it was not going to touch me.'

How did he take it? 'I was angry with God,' he continued. 'I am a Roman Catholic. I felt this was God's punishment... Give me a second chance. Let this be a mistake and I will reform myself. I was angry with everyone, including myself.'

And then Dominic Marcus D'Souza left his body.

I am in Panaji, in the parlour of Don Bosco school where Dominic studied. Classes are over for the day. Large shadows and a dark silence stalk the corridors. What was Dominic like? I am curious. Was he a happy child or did misfortune call on him early in life? 'Dominic was in Uganda as a child. He was twelve years old when he came to India. He was six years older than me but we used to meet as friends. He was my neighbour at Parra,' says Loretta Pinto. 'He was outgoing, very lively and mischievous. He was a good hockey player, a good athlete and also good at studies. We acted in a play together and he was terrific. He always used to make people laugh.'

Isabelle Vaz, a slim and well-spoken teacher at the school, organizes a theatre company called The Mustard Seed for which Dominic frequently performed. 'We always thought that AIDS was a gay white man's disease,' she tells me. 'When it came to Parra the reaction was one of shock. At that time we didn't think of the consequences. We just thought that it was a friend who needed help. We didn't know it was Dominic. He should never have been treated that way.' Mario Coelho, who acted with him, is filled with praise for Dominic. 'He pushed himself very hard. He was full of life even after testing positive. He lived without regrets.'

Tamsin Charrier, another beautiful admirer of Dominic, was with him till the very end. When she talks, her eyes well up with tears. We take a long walk away from school as the evening breeze settles in, on one of the less-crowded little lanes. 'We first met in a play. We became friends instantly,' she says. 'You could say that I was an intimate friend. My relationship with Dominic had nothing to do with his being HIV-positive. Dominic is not "was", he "is". I feel that something about Dominic is still with us. As far as I am concerned he is still with me.'

Friends in the The Mustard Seed vividly recall Dominic's acting skills. 'In the theatre group the quality of his support was a great source of strength,' remembers Isabelle. 'He had this splendid presence on stage. He was radiant. We miss him. He could be harsh, critical, blunt, irritable, but never to hurt. Once we did *Jonathan Livingston Seagull*. Dominic was the seagull. Even now when I see a bird I think of him. He worked very hard. He recited his lines even when he rode his bike. Even in isolation he was planning another play. He had such a creative mind and such a free spirit.'

Later, on another day, I drive down to Baina, the red-light area of Goa, slightly beyond the fringes of Vasco. It is a long drive from Panaji. I have been to several flesh districts but this one was marked by the smell of dry excreta. I am told later that the huge public toilet close by has had no water supply for over a week. Most of the sex workers in Baina are from south India. The bars and the cubicles are filled with personnel from docked ships. The latest rock numbers ricochet from the walls like a background score to herald the grand entry of sexual disease. Children of sex workers play in nearby swamps as their mothers entertain boisterous and gaudily tattooed clients.

'I met Dominic at a play we were in together,' says the attractive and wildly engaging Shaila D'Souza, a social worker in Baina. 'I read about Dominic being HIV-positive in the papers. I thought it was someone else. I contacted friends who told me that it was "our Dominic". I went to see him at the little room in the sanatorium. It had a guard outside. Until I saw him I couldn't understand the trauma he was going through. He was very brave. At that time I realized the strength he had. I wouldn't have been able to handle it.'

The next day I drop by at Dominic's house at Parra to meet Lucy, his mother, petite and pleasant, dressed in a yellow frock. She is a nurse and is leaving for a house visit when I drop in unannounced. But she is all smiles and welcomes me with tea and ginger biscuits. 'Dominic was a very loving child,' she begins. 'He always wanted to be with me. He would come running to me after school and hold my hand, unlike his twin brother who was rough and tough. He was fond of animals and babies and was surrounded by girls. When he started going to college he was always giving the girls a lift on his motorbike. He was a good sportsman and never had a medical problem.'

It is obvious that Dominic was mummy's pet. 'I liked him more than I liked Cedric. Even the priests at school were fond of him.

They wanted him to join the priesthood. There is nothing I didn't like about him.' When he was found to be HIV-positive, Lucy was surprised. 'I follow the Catholic religion and prayed a lot at that time. I put all my trust in Him. That helped.'

How did the rest of the family react? 'My daughter is in Kenya, the eldest son is in Canada and Dominic's twin brother is in Sweden. They are all married with their own families. They were shocked and sad. They came to see Dominic in turns. My son-in-law came from Kenya for the funeral. My daughter came later.' Lucy never saw Dominic worried or discouraged. 'Even towards the end, when he was deteriorating in health, he didn't give up hope. He became a bit pensive though. He wanted to help all HIV people. That became an obsession.'

After Dominic lost his job, Claude Alvares, a well-known writer and environmentalist, and his wife, Norma, offered him one at their Goa Foundation. 'We never knew Dominic before,' admits Norma over fruit juice one late evening in their newly constructed home near Parra. 'We came to know of him only through the papers – the HIV case. Everybody said that he was educated and decent. That's all we knew. Then we met and he came home too. He struck me as confident, able and as one who could get along with others. He was also a good worker.'

Claude chips in, 'He began working with us gradually. He used to work on the computer at home. Then he came to the office. He disarmed everybody in the office with his remarkably loving personality.' Dominic evidently had a way with people. 'Even the servant cried so much when he died,' remembers Norma. 'She loved feeding him. She knew nothing about HIV or his illness. Dominic used to take her on his bike to the market for shopping.'

Dominic surprised everyone with his incredible resilience. 'He was never sick during the entire period he was with us,' adds Norma. 'He was never bitter or sad. The only thing he was careful about was to keep his head covered in the rainy season. He didn't want to catch a cold and get some other complications. But he never wanted to go home early or anything like that. He hated being mollycoddled. In fact, we took strength from him whenever we had a problem. He was the best ambassador HIV people could have.'

Dominic's first trip to Amsterdam for an AIDS conference changed him. 'It was a turning point,' recollects Norma. 'Till that time he was very quiet about being HIV-positive. After the trip he was ready to announce it publicly.' Dominic helped Norma and Claude with outdoor work and with book publishing. He read proofs, designed pages and liaised with printers. 'The work was very different from what he was used to,' says Claude. 'But we gave him total freedom and there was no cause for complaint. He worked hard.'

In the beginning, the local press sensationalized the issue. A Goan AIDS patient, the first in India, was too juicy a topic for the provincial press to let pass. 'The local press was simply not equipped to handle the enormity of the situation,' says journalist and poet Manohar Shetty. He remembers meeting Dominic. 'He was a warm and friendly person. There was no bitterness in him. It was a very difficult time. Dominic bore the brunt of all the ostracism well.'

Dominic's was a short and eventful life, and one of great purpose. 'Looking at it from the Public Health Act, it was an eyeopener,' says Dr. I.S. Gilada, who spearheaded the campaign for his release, acceptance and treatment. 'For the first time the Public Health Act became public. The Act had a provision for the mandatory isolation of all HIV-positive people, whether Goan or outsiders. As a result of the Dominic case, HIV-positive people are no longer isolated.'

Before Dominic D'Souza happened, all the HIV cases in Goa were those of foreigners and they just flew back home. The Goa health authorities were smug in the mistaken belief that no Goenkar would ever test positive. In the battle against AIDS, particularly in India, the Dominic D'Souza phase is of more than ordinary importance. It was thanks to him that Positive People (a group which encouraged HIV-positive people to air their concerns) was started, a Draconian piece of legislation (which saw Dominic in jail) amended, and India sensitized to the issue of AIDS. All future intervention projects have picked up the baton from Dominic.

The last will and testament of Dominic Marcus D'Souza made at the Breach Candy hospital in Mumbai on May 23, 1992, four days before his death, read:

Should I die in Bombay, I would prefer my body to be cremated and the ashes to be sent to Goa. And if I die in Goa, only the neighbours and my closest friends will be informed of the funeral. There will be no newspaper announcement. The newspaper announcement will come after the funeral and will boldly say that I died of AIDS and that I am not ashamed to say it. My funeral must be a very simple one with no band at all, no fire crackers, and a cheap, poor man's coffin. If I die in Goa, I should be buried as soon as possible. And all the formalities of informing family can be attended to immediately after the funeral.

Nineteen years have passed since Dominic passed on the baton. Nineteen years is a long time. Long enough for India to set in place the machinery required for treatment and solace.

The child shall be protected against all forms of neglect, cruelty and exploitation.
He/she shall not be the subject of traffic, in any form.
        —Principle 9 of the Declaration of the Rights of the Child
          proclaimed by the United Nations General Assembly on
                    20 November 1959: Resolution 1386 (XIV)

In 1982, Tulasa Thapa, a young girl of thirteen, was rescued from the brothels of Mumbai. Her frail body was broken into little pieces by three venereal diseases and three types of tuberculosis. She was treated in a local hospital, massive efforts were made to contact her family in Nepal and, finally, she was sent back home. Hundreds of thousands of young girls find employment in the flesh districts of India but, as was the case with Dominic D'Souza, the rescue and rehabilitation of Tulasa Thapa became another significant milestone in India's battle against AIDS and exploitation. Someone had to stand up to highlight the issue. In this case, Dominic and Tulasa inadvertently became the pall-bearers of the cause.

The Tulasa case was an eye opener. She became a symbol of hope for the little girls languishing in the debauchery and depravation of the Indian street. Women were being trafficked into India from Nepal in large numbers. Thanks to her, both governments looked at the issue with some concern and several campaigns were initiated to stem the flow. A lot has changed but a lot remains to be done. In retrospect, Dominic and Tulasa, in their own differing contexts, became the faces of the new thrust for justice.

In 1994, twelve years after her rescue, I went to Nepal on a mission: to search for Tulasa Thapa. I had heard that she was still alive, but where in Nepal? I had no clue. Not much was known of her since her departure from India. I worked on a few leads thrown at me in tiny morsels, like a challenging jigsaw puzzle, and finally ferreted her out. But, before that, there is an interesting tale to tell. This distraction from the narration is essential to understand how India works.

In 1993, Mumbai was torn apart by serial bombs. Several clues and names emerged from the debris of (mis)information. A certain Tiger Memon was named as one of the suspects and there was an Interpol alert for him. While I waited at the check-in counter at the Mumbai airport, I tried to hook my antennae on various levels of corruption that normally sweep an Indian airport. Today, eighteen years later, Indian airports look much better and the blatant misappropriation of basic ethics is not flaunted openly. But in those days they enriched tomes on corruption with great passion.

The man in front of me in the queue was a poor labourer going to Dubai. The police officer in charge examined his passport and made sure that he would get loads of gifts from him on his return. The labourer, who was on a tourist visa, had his local address taken down and was also asked to part with money. So he politely placed a few hundred rupees between the leaves of the passport and the officer on duty pocketed them without a pause. The cop also gave him a personal shopping list. All this was in the late afternoon, under the gaze of powerful tube lights, a few feet away from me.

Now it was my turn. I was excitedly waiting for the officer to ask me for a bribe. It had happened many times before and I just loved the exchanges. He took my passport, held it in front of him at different angles and kept staring at me. This went on for close to ten minutes and I was getting impatient. If he was gay, I wanted to tell him that I wasn't.

He then pounced on me, held me by my collar and asked me my name. I told him my name and then, irritated, told him that it was also written on my passport and that it would be a good idea if the authorities could replace him with an officer who could read simple English. He then asked me all the details that the passport carried about me. Not keen on creating a scene, I answered politely. He then heaved me away roughly. 'Come,' he said, not letting go of my collar. I played along without protest. It is against the law to hit a man in uniform. I was taken to a separate enclave and made to sit under armed guard. I was wondering what had happened. After a few minutes, a senior officer approached me and said curtly, 'You can go now.' My passport was also handed back to me. When

I asked him what the matter was, he explained that the officer on duty thought I was Tiger Memon! Now I couldn't continue being polite. I went up to him and said, 'Buddy, if I was Tiger Memon you would be licking my boots like a pussy cat. If only you had gone to school, you would have realized the difference between Menon (my surname in the passport) and Memon.' Before he could retaliate, I flashed my press card and the black dye nearly fell off the dirty toothbrush on his upper lip.

This detour from the Tulasa files is important. The Indian police are notorious and will not stop at anything. They are intricately woven with crime. If you are poor, without contacts and unable to fight for your rights, they will make stew out of you. The sex worker, as you can well imagine, has no chance.

Tulasa Thapa never had a chance!

Kathmandu takes its own time to even warm up to a time warp. Opulent hotels, several eateries and markets oozing with exotic bric-a-brac are flush with tourists. Nepal hasn't been taken over by any country in particular but by the whole world. The Indians have a huge business presence and the West is at the vanguard of all international philanthropy. So Nepal, as a poor nation, is always at the receiving end.

Kathmandu has grand casinos, beautiful houses and vestiges of the good life. Like other poor nations, Nepal too suffers from widespread inequity. Poverty is everywhere. Nepal has the Living Goddesss but the dollar is the living god. Tourists from all over the world crowd Nepal. It is cheap, lives in the mists of time and affords breathtaking trekking trails. It is also strategically placed. You can peep into India, Tibet, China and the Himalayas with just a turn of the head.

There are other distractions too. You can watch soccer matches and stare at the same time at the snow gently melting on mountain peaks. It is also a good place to check out the latest offerings that take ecstasy to new highs. The Durbar Square used to rock once. It was attached to a road named Freak Street in homage to all the freaks that made it their rendezvous with such gusto in the good old days of free love and anti-war protest. The glitz has now moved to Thamel. Just say aloud your fondest desires and Thamel, like a genie, will deliver. Stray away from the capital and you can feast on the ancient towns of Bhaktapur and Patan. Wander around a bit more, take rickety rides out of the city and get on to sheer trails up mountain slopes conquered only by Sherpas and sure-footed goats. There is insurgency now, there have been several political upheavals, and the monarchy has lost its popularity. But these are just wrinkles on the beautiful face of paradise. It is still awash in the cuddle of Himalayan sunlight.

I had to work fast. Tulasa was somewhere in Nepal and I had to get to her before she moved out or fell seriously sick. I made contact with organizations working in the trafficking of women. Word got around that a journalist from Mumbai was looking for Tulasa Thapa. People volunteered information. Finally, in less than a week, I found her.

'My father doesn't meet me. My stepmother hates me. My stomach pains all the time and I am bound to this wheelchair. I have never cheated anybody. Why has all this happened to me? Is it my karma?' Tulasa cries out to me in pain. Her sparse frame, then twenty-four years old, broken by disease and premature ageing, shudders and shakes in the wheelchair that gives her the freedom to move. We are at the Cheshire Home in Jorpatti, some 20 kilometres from Kathmandu's busy marketplace. Other residents of the home, all physically and emotionally broken, stare at us with curiosity. Who is this man from Mumbai, they wonder. Is he a piece from Tulasa's past, her saviour or one who has sinned?

Washed in spotless white, the Cheshire Home sits squat in the centre of several acres of land far away from the pollution of the city, cradled by a garden of seasonal flowers smiling at the sun. From the tiny, barred window in Tulasa's room, one can see towering mountain peaks scratching the cloudless sky. There is nothing else for miles on end. An airplane or a stray cloud may pass by. It is such a beautiful day.

Tulasa's cry wanders across the rectangular courtyard, past the flowers gently swaying in the breeze and into the rarified mountain air. But there are no takers. She will have to make friends with her loneliness, with the pain and sorrow that have nestled in her bones. She will have to live with memories that tear her insides and singe her soul with Satanic cruelty.

Tulasa is one of thousands of teenagers abducted from home in Nepal and sold to the brothels of India every year. Most of them slither into the sordid holds of complete decadence. Those who are found to be HIV-positive are sent back. The others just drift into oblivion, mangled by the crushing nexus of the police, the pimp and the politician. Now they are all dying of AIDS.

Tulasa was abducted from Thankut village in Bagmati district near Kathmandu and smuggled to Mumbai through Birganj. She was sold thrice to different brothels for a few thousand rupees each time. Brutalized and ravaged, it was only when her diseased body was rushed to hospital that her ordeal miraculously came to an end. A local NGO salvaged whatever remained of her, secured medical attention, contacted her father in Nepal, and sent her home. The rescue operation took months. Tulasa's story hovered on the bestseller list all along with poignant narrations of a life of continued and relentless exploitation.

According to Tulasa, she was returning home from an errand when an acquaintance chatted her up and then just smuggled her across the border into India. He was not alone. There were accomplices. It was well planned. She was thrashed into abject submission. In Mumbai, she was sold to Tuli, a brothel-keeper, who used her and then sold her to Rita, another madam, for a profit. Tulasa was sold a third time to a brothel-keeper named Gauri. The debauchery continued till she was crushed body and soul.

In hospital, Tulasa spoke of her days in hell. Police collusion with the flesh trade was high on her list of revelations. She named people and helped locate brothels. But after her departure for Nepal, her story came to an end. The Tulasa files shut as dramatically as they had opened. The flesh trade continued without a pause. It just ironed out the loopholes, got more streamlined, made sure that there would be no further glitches, and gained momentum. More girls were trafficked and supply managed to keep pace with demand.

At twenty-four, Tulasa is in the autumn of her life. She is strapped to a wheelchair with only painful memories for company. Soon after her abduction, her mother died of shock, her stepmother wanted nothing to do with her and her father, possibly keen on maintaining peace at home, avoided looking for her. Her great dismay, more intense than the pain that is tearing her body in ribbons, is the thought that she has been used as a commodity and never been loved for the person that she is. 'I am ready to marry,' she tells me weakly, looking into my eyes and straining at the strap confining her to the wheelchair. 'If there is a nice man who will accept me. I will tell him everything.' And then she smiles, a trifle shy. The smile spreads across her face like gathering dawn and slowly lightens the pain in her eyes.

'I was cheated,' Tulasa repeats over and over again. 'Eight girls were cheated but we are all back in Nepal now. The boys responsible for this are in jail in Kathmandu. My father caught them.' She rambles a lot. Most of the time she is incoherent and talks nonsense. There is a dribble from her mouth, she wipes it off, and clutches her stomach and winces. Then she cries. The doctors attending on her say that she has severe psychological problems. That is only to be expected, they say. 'She desperately wants to be loved and cherished as a human being but her family just doesn't care. We have spoken to them but they just don't want to visit her.'

Tulasa has been at the Cheshire Home for several years. A small and committed medical staff attends on her and the other residents with love and concern. But there is no provision for an indefinite stay. 'We can't keep her endlessly,' say the doctors. 'There are others needing attention and this is not a hostel. But if nobody wants her what do we do, where do we send her?' Tulasa shares her room with another girl. It is a large and clean room with light green walls and two cots with attached cupboards stacked against two corners, one for each girl. She opens a cupboard and shows me a letter from a social worker in Mumbai. 'He loves me very much,' she says. 'He also comes to see me.'

We move to the courtyard. The air is crisp and scented with the fragrance of different flowers. 'My stomach pains all the time,' continues Tulasa. 'I can't even go to the toilet. There is nothing in my life, absolutely nothing. Why has my life been like this? Why has all this happened to me?' She starts weeping inconsolably. 'I hate Mumbai. I hate everything about it. I remember everything so clearly. My life there was a nightmare. Arabs, Indians, white people, policemen, everybody used me. Sometimes they took me to a big hotel by the sea. I cried every night. I wanted to run away. But where could I go? I was so young then. And who could I go to for help?'

Dr I.S. Gilada, responsible for Tulasa's rescue, remembers her vividly. His NGO had organized a camp with sex workers in Mumbai's red-light area in June 1982. It was the first of several incursions into the world of prostitution. They found Tulasa stricken with syphilis, gonorrhoea, venereal warts and different types of tuberculosis. She was saved, admitted to hospital and a full-fledged 'Save Tulasa' campaign launched. A police complaint was made and with startling speed thirty-two persons, including the three brothel-owners named by Tulasa, arrested. 'You see, the police know exactly what is going on,' Dr Gilada told me later.

Tulasa made headlines. The media gobbled up her story without exhaustion. Out of fear of reprisals, she was given police protection, sent to a remand home and then brought back for further treatment. The newspapers in Nepal latched on to the story and Tulasa's father came to Mumbai to take her back. The police cut off their friendship bands with the traffickers and several arrests were made. India and Nepal also signed a treaty in 1985 for the rescue and repatriation of Nepali girls languishing in the brothels of India.

The abductors of Tulasa were given twenty years in jail. Abduction laws were made more stringent in Nepal and the government embarked on a programme to educate local panchayats on the evils of prostitution and the need to prevent the sale of young girls. For the first time, in the long, dark and evil history of flesh trade in the subcontinent, child prostitution and the abduction and forced sale of women hogged time, space and redressal.

Tulasa's father, Dhoj Thapa, wrote an emotional letter to the doctor attending on her in Mumbai:

'Sir, yesterday, on the 14th of October 1984, after three long years, I took my daughter into my custody from the Nepalese police. In place of a healthy, laughing twelve-year-old child I got back a crippled, ailing fifteen-year-old shadow of a girl, mute in tears of fear and anguish to see her father and home once again. As you know, Tulasa lost her mother just six months after her kidnapping from Kathmandu. There is no mother to take her back into her protective arms. With all this pain, agony and suffering, all she brought back with her is a pair of crutches without which she cannot move.'

Offers of monetary and emotional aid poured in from all over the world. And Tulasa finally went back to Nepal.

We have been chatting for a while now. From her wheelchair, Tulasa stares into the distance. Her eyes are large, lonely, lost and dead. Her gaze wanders into the mountains, and beyond. She still clutches her stomach in pain, but it's her broken soul that lashes out at the world. Will justice ever be done? Was she born only to be sold and resold, to be tortured and damned, to be raped and never loved, and condemned to die while still in the prime of life? Why was she chosen so longingly by misery as its handmaiden? What was the purpose of this indignity called life that was heaped on her without permission? And if all that happened to her was in judgement, then judgement for what?

There are no answers. The darkness is settling in. Small lamps are lit and a prayer session begins. Everybody joins in.

I step out. There is a lump in my throat. I cannot pray.

I leave the Cheshire Home and return to my digs in Kathmandu. After a wash, I walk over to one of the restaurants off Durbar Square and grab a drink. The food is excellent and the restaurant is buzzing with the energy of young Westerners seeking out adventure in the crisp Himalayan air. I stagger back to my room very late in the night, recklessly evading boisterous street traffic, and sleep with a thousand knives.

At Patan, the next day, away from street noises, in a closet of green, I meet up with Sangeeta, Saira, Kamala, Suntali and Chameli. They will die very soon. They are HIV-positive sex workers, just out of their teens. They have been sent back to Nepal from the brothels of Mumbai. The last trails of life ooze out of their pores.

Suntali is in the final stages. Her skin has aged overnight. It is dark, pigmented, hard and scaly like sandpaper. She is losing weight rapidly, looks drawn and withered and is host to many infections. There is also the overpowering stench of decay, of rotting, that emanates from her. She is just nineteen. The others are also about the same age. None of them talks much. They just look at each other in silence. What is there to say? Crickets call out to each other in the garden outside. It is the same story. Of being cheated, sold and ravaged. With AIDS, the old story has a new sting.

They look on helplessly. No one wants to die. Even if it has been a terrible life, even if all their dreams have been amputated in the womb, they wait everyday so eagerly for the warm glisten of sunshine. It is so honest. It greets you without prejudice or opinion with its quiet, golden spread. Just like the morning dew and the soft quiver of the breeze. So giving of its purity. Everywhere flowers are in bloom and the silence of passing clouds is wondrous. Despite it all, it is still a beautiful life. Death will take it all away. No, they don't want to die.

'Your government should do something about all this,' says Dr Purnima Gurung of the Community Health Development Centre (CHDC), where the girls are housed. 'They should be medically checked in India. They should be given some money, better food, better treatment. They are used like animals. We hear that there are thousands of sex workers in the red-light area in Bombay. Why doesn't your government make prostitution legal and provide proper medical assistance?'

The community centre is clean and Spartan. Like all the other rehabilitation homes, it also has a large heart. The girls receive more love than they have ever known. But there is very little time that they can call their own. Every valuable second that passes steals the last heartbeats of life. A few jokes are thrown in now and then and there is laughter. But a deep melancholy courses through it all. How can that be painted in another colour?

'HIV is becoming a big problem here,' continues Dr Gurung. 'It is increasing every day. Most of our girls are sold to the Bombay markets. They come back here to die with AIDS. The girls are from the villages. They are ignorant. They know nothing. They are brought to the carpet factories as cheap labour and then lured to India. Bombay is the hot spot.' Dr Gurung has been a social worker for many years. She has a nursing home and a rehabilitation centre and the kind manners of one who has seen a lot and is humbled by it. She instinctively empathizes with suffering. The phone rings. 'We will be getting another AIDS case soon,' she says after a short conversation. 'God, when will this stop?'

Back in Mumbai, I visit the red-light areas. Nothing has changed. Business is brisk as ever. The brothels are overflowing with younger flesh. There are more Nepali women. Later, the newspapers carry a brief report stating that Tulasa Thapa has died. Not many see it. It goes unnoticed. Ever since she left Mumbai, other girls had taken their positions in the brothels. The script left unfinished by Tulasa will be choreographed with more sorrow.

We must accept finite disappointment, but never lose infinite hope.
—Martin Luther King Jr

In countries like India, where food, clothing and shelter remain beyond the reach of most people and where old epidemics in new clothes revisit with uncanny regularity, the battle against AIDS can be lost even before the first slingshots are readied. As most of us who live in this part of the world know only too well, even our fire-fighting techniques are obsolete. But, surprisingly, despite habitual procrastination on sensitive issues that need urgent repair, the Government of India has stretched itself on this issue. Systems have been readied and battle stations prepared. The immediacy of the situation has magically reached home.

All blood is now screened for HIV, professional blood donation has been disallowed by legislation, infected pregnant women have access to medicines, sex education has been introduced in schools, alternate sexuality is being viewed with less alarm, condoms are distributed free in the flesh districts, the female condom has been selectively introduced, hospices are being set up, and India has emerged as one of the largest manufacturers of the highly active anti-retroviral therapy (HAART) with a surplus that eyes foreign markets. It is also believed to be close to discovering a conventional and affordable treatment for AIDS with minimal side effects. No medico-social challenge in India has ever been addressed as seriously as AIDS has. It has rocked the front pages and hogged precious time on television and radio, and an entire generation of professionals is working overtime to get a fix on the problem. Indigenous vaccine initiatives have been launched, and with the advent of the HIV, a new era in medical jurisprudence has taken birth.

Every effort is being made to stem its spread. There's a good chance that India won't allow HIV to blow up its innards like it has done in other parts of the world.

I meet up again with John Frederick, the tall, slim, bespectacled American who is the guru of the street. He knows more about prostitution and trafficking of women than entire governments. We have worked together in the past and decide to check out Kamathipura. We had heard that it was now living in fear after massive police crackdowns. John has come down from Nepal where he runs an NGO called Ray of Hope.

We meet up at his lodging house in Colaba and take a cab to Kamathipura. We check out old places together; we have known several sex workers in the area well and we have gifts and words of encouragement for them. Pimps follow us with great hope. John is a 'white' man and I look like I have just walked out of a merchant vessel docked in Mumbai harbour. We are choice targets. The pimps surround us. Most of them are alcoholics and drug addicts and refuse to believe that we are not flesh shoppers.

Kamathipura has changed a lot from the early days. It has been badly kicked in the butt. First, HIV latched on, and now the police have become more aggressive spurred on by pressure from human rights organizations. Quite rightly, there is a watch on children and teenagers entering the profession. But now there are no customers either. They get mopped up in police raids and don't want to take a chance. As a result, rates have fallen and the women are more desperate. There is talk of leaving the area and moving to other places. New red-light areas are mushrooming all over the city.

We talk to Jaya, in her twenties, thin, tall and acne-marked, nervously standing on the road in a black saree with blue dots, close to a police outpost. She is a 'floater'. She doesn't belong to a brothel but has visiting rights. If she picks up a customer, she can take him to a brothel that she has struck a deal with.

Jaya hasn't had a customer for days. She is worried. There is no money for the family and she doesn't know what to do or where to go. She also has a lot of competition and there are hundreds like her on the street unprotected by the collective economics of a brothel. Her rates are rock bottom now, and she is not standing here, in the noise of traffic and pollution, warding off disease and destitution with all her prayers, for free sex.

We continue walking through the maze of lanes and head back. There is nothing to say. Harsh walls of silence accompany us on the journey home.

CHAPTER 8

ESCAPADES

Make voyages! – Attempt them! – there's nothing else...
—Tennessee Williams

I was in Kolkata several years ago covering its rich street life. After weeks of ribald adventure, I decided to look up an old friend now betrothed for life to the Indian Administrative Service. He was my colleague in Mumbai's leading newspaper when he chose the security of employment with the government over the uncertain life of a hack. I rang him up for directions and he insisted that I drop by immediately. 'I am a government servant,' he yelled happily on a bad line. 'There is never any work. Just drop in and you will have the key to the city.' I was with him in an hour.

We packed up soon after. Kolkata had a power shortage and even office gossip got tedious in the humid room and in the poor light of old lanterns. We got into his chauffeur-driven white Ambassador and decided to go to an inexpensive but good Chinese eatery where we talked about old times. A few drinks down the throat, and it was already early evening. Kolkata was slumming away, as always. 'What are your plans now?' my friend asked. 'Come with me to Sonagachi. I will introduce you to a world you have never dreamt of.' Sonagachi is the traditional red-light district of Kolkata.

It was dark when we reached Sonagachi. The traffic crawled and the power crisis had swallowed several parts of the city. We stopped the car a little before our destination and sent the driver home. We didn't want him squealing the next day. We walked through narrow lanes and climbed the steep stairs of one of the many dilapidated buildings. My friend led the way. He knew every pebble even if its back was turned on us.

We entered a large room on the third floor of an old building embraced by the fragrance of jasmine and the strains of Pandit Ravishankar. An emaciated stray dog at the steps saw us, dug its tail deep between its legs and slunk away nervously. And there she was, an apparition waiting for my friend, adorned in chiffon and marigold. They had been lovers for several years, a relationship he preserved even after an elaborate arranged marriage and two children. 'Everything is on the house, do what you want,' said my friend, slapping me on my back. He was well known in Sonagachi. And then he disappeared into one of the rooms with his lady for the rest of the night.

I looked around. There were beautiful women on low-flung divans. I was told that every intoxicant was also available. Since I had nothing better to do and was assured that no money would spill out of my meagre hack's salary, I accompanied one of the girls to a large room with a huge black and white television with scratches as offerings from the state-owned broadcaster. We got drinks and I listened to the girl play the tanpura. She sang old Bengali songs, throwing out the words like 'rosagullas' from a crimson-kissed mouth. After several songs and drinks, she accepted her fate for the night. She must have concluded that her friend's paramour had brought along a eunuch for safety. As the hours passed I couldn't make out if she was singing or yawning. All I could see was that she kept opening her mouth. I was too tired and drunk to notice much more. Early morning my friend leapt into the room and woke me up. Having had a marvellous time, he tipped everybody in the brothel well, kissed his lady goodbye, promised to return soon, and we descended the long flight of stairs. In the emerging light of daybreak the lanes were a confusing maze but my friend was sure that he knew his way to the car. He had done this before. We had just stepped out of Sonagachi when suddenly, out of nowhere, like a guerilla attack, thousands of people descended on us. They were shouting slogans, carrying lanterns and waving flags. They surrounded us. We were terrified. Did the driver guess what his boss was up to and spill the beans? Would the government dismiss my friend from service? Would we be lynched by the mob? Was it the moral brigade, all furious and ready to punish us? We stood there bewildered. We couldn't run away. The mob had choked all exits. There was fury and agitation in their body language. They raised fists and shouted slogans. We waited patiently for the death sentence. Maybe, we thought, the time had come to leave this world with whatever dignity we could afford after, what could politely be called, a late night.

Finally, the sloganeering came to a halt and a dark, skinny gent in kurta pyjama and thick black spectacles and black rubber chappals approached us. He was the leader of the group. Our fate in Sonagachi rested in his hands. He looked at us and smiled benignly from under a thick black moustache. Then he thrust a three-page memorandum under our noses and asked us, in Bengali, to sign. We were ready to do anything to get out of the place alive. We would have signed on his underwear if he had even whispered a request. He told us that they were resisting the Russian intervention in Afghanistan and that they were enlisting support. 'Afghanistan should be untouched and left free,' they told us. If we signed up we would automatically qualify as sympathizers of a common cause. We signed without more prodding, shook hands, congratulated them on their sensitivity to such international causes, and quietly slipped away.

Kolkata is full of surprises.

On another visit, while investigating the Bangladeshi exodus into the city, I sniffed out a procurer in the market and followed him like a terrier. He had slipped into Kolkata from Bangladesh without papers and was working as a pimp and kidnapper. If the money was good, he told me, he would also kill. He needed to start life from scratch and anything that allowed him to do that was most welcome. He was in a dirty lungi, banian and sandals. He had the look of a man who had been on death row for several generations; one among so many who had been condemned in this life by an overload of karmic destitution.

I normally sense danger very fast, and I did this time too, but I was so excited by my find that I didn't listen to the signals. I just wanted to know more about how the Bangladeshis lived in India. I followed him to another dilapidated building. Years of communist rule in Kolkata had preserved it for a life of poverty. The city was a gigantic slum going to seed with some purpose. We went up to the second floor and he introduced me to two of the worst-looking women ever!

They had over two hundred pounds in all the wrong places, pus oozed out of their eyes and they could barely see. I thought their movements were directed solely by their olfactory skills. They also smelt like dead bodies. I now knew what he was up to. I complimented him on his taste in women and added that maybe I should check them out another day. He missed the sarcasm and called out for more women. One look and they could have crippled the Cyclops.

I told him not to work so hard, to take a well-deserved break, and that I would return over the weekend. I tried to tell him that

146

pimping wasn't a blue-chip profession and wouldn't be for some time if the law had its way. But he kept looking at me with venom and insisted that I listen to him. 'Choose any girl,' he screamed, throwing out spittle.

Clearly unused to a sense of humour and lacking basic courtesies, he caught me by the neck, pushed me against the wall, levelled his knee at my crotch in attack mode, pulled a naked razor out and asked me to cough up all my money and jewellery, or else. He could have cut short the speech; the body language was strong enough. I wear several good-luck pendants. I had no choice.

The room was large, without windows, and had a wooden door that made it look like a medieval dungeon. He stood facing me against the door that was both exit and entrance. I gave him all the money and jewellery I had. As a bribe, I even gave him a few useless suburban train tickets from Mumbai that the dhobi failed to pick out of my pant pockets. He was too illiterate to know that they were of no value. He looked at my socks and shoes greedily but they didn't smell or look too good with all the street goo on them. Finally, with what I thought was a long sigh, he gave up on further dreams of sartorial acquisition.

He grabbed all that he could without question and still kept the knife at my throat. The knee relaxed a bit. 'Stay here,' he commanded. I reasoned that since I had given him what he had asked for, I was free to leave. He was evidently not keen on keeping his end of the deal. I could see that he wasn't a man of integrity or great intelligence. He slapped my face and pressed the knife harder. People go missing in India every day for less profound reasons. I knew that he could do anything to me. I could be killed and dumped into some room and even the cockroaches wouldn't find me for years.

I was desperate. I had been in difficult situations before but this was different. I should have listened to my gut feeling, but now it was too late. The women were advancing towards me. I was sure it was the shoes. I recoiled and wondered what to do. Luckily for me, the women got into a discussion with the procurer that grew into a heated argument. Maybe, he hadn't shared the booty with them. Distracted, he eased the knife from my throat. This was my only chance. I had to grab the split second.

I lunged at one of the women. She fell on the procurer, who fell on the other woman. They lay in a mountainous heap of flesh and ooze like an erupting volcano on its backside. I jumped over the sprawled bodies and made for the door. He tried to get up but I sent a power-packed upper cut to his distorted jaw. He wasn't Adonis by any stretch of imagination and any alteration to his looks would have suited him. In the bargain, I gained a few seconds.

It all happened in an instant. The procurer recovered and raised an alarm. Reinforcements darted in from other rooms. I saw the challenge and leapt off the second floor to land squarely on my feet. There was another Bangladeshi manning the exit but he was half asleep. By the time he opened his eyes wide, I had knocked him silly. He passed out without his lungi, lying on his back in torn, striped underwear. I blasted through the main door and landed on the street at the front wheel of a passing scooter that screeched to a halt a hair's breadth from my face. Looking back, I realize that I could have made it in Hindi cinema as a stuntman or extra if the hack's union had forbidden me from writing another word. But it wasn't at all funny then.

'Where are the police?' I screamed. 'I am a journalist. I want the police.' People gathered around us, and the commotion was attracting large numbers of passers-by. The owner of the tiny Bajaj scooter, a large, corpulent fellow in white shirt and black striped pants, sensing the folly of the moment, quietly whisked me away. We went to a teashop close by where I explained what had happened. 'Don't worry,' he comforted me. 'I am a lawyer and you are a journalist and we know how the police work. So there is no point going to them. Let me handle this. I know the area.'

We returned to the den and the lawyer summoned the owner. They discussed my case as though it had come up for final hearing at the high court. The owner seemed completely embarrassed by all this. He apologized, brought the procurer, made him return all that he had taken, slapped him, told him to kiss my feet and ask for pardon, which he did, and then I was given the grand option of choosing any woman I wanted in the brothel for as long as I wanted her without having to pay. Even this beat had a freebie!

The owner told me that it was a privilege that a journalist had come to his workspace and that he was terribly upset that I wasn't accorded the honour I deserved. He slapped the procurer again, who was now grovelling at my feet. He also kicked him in the ribs to confirm his allegiance to me. I had had enough. I thanked them all, told the owner that I would be back very soon, hired a tired cab and sped away as fast and as far as I could.

Much later, back in Mumbai, I was doing a story on hijras. The monsoon was petering to a slow halt. The rains had left the bowels of the city damp and wheezing like a chronic asthmatic. Mounds of garbage in the flesh district had now spread out evenly on the road without the help of the municipality. The road looked and smelt like it had been bathed in a venomous mix of new and old excreta, plastic and stale food marinated at great expense with a World Bank loan, thanks to some clever lobbying by the external affairs ministry. Even deep breathing was difficult. Yet, the streets were packed with flesh shoppers.

I found a home of hijras close to the Delhi Durbar, one of the more flamboyant eateries in the area and a landmark of Mumbai. It is an old and spacious restaurant serving Mughal delicacies. The Delhi Durbar can house hundreds of customers at any given time and is open till the early hours of the morning. Surrounding it, on both sides of the lane, young human flesh is sold for less than the cost of a large plate of chicken biryani consisting of one frail leg piece, some rice in gravy, potatoes and white onion sliced in weak curd and offered on greasy ceramic plates.

I walked in and said a cheery hello. When you are on this beat, a sense of humour is always handy. The dark, dirty room, on the second floor of a ruin, housed a dozen hijras. I kept looking at the ceiling, hoping it wouldn't come crashing down on my long, shampooed hair. Tall, dark, almost as black as the night, and well built, the hijras clapped their hands deliriously in welcome.

I sat down carefully, asked a few questions and realized that I wasn't making any headway. One of the rafters holding up the ceiling was also trembling and it was making me more nervous. So I decided to leave. That's when they got aggressive. 'You are leaving,' they exclaimed in shock. 'Why? Don't you like us?' I told them that they were gorgeous and just what I needed on a day like this but I had to leave on another appointment. 'I will come again,' I promised.

'But you can't go just like that,' they countered. 'How much money do you have? Give it to us.' The handclapping got furious and they advanced towards me in a circle. They must have played kabbadi as kids.

Again, I had to move fast. This was becoming the leitmotif of my existence. I leapt at the cordon, broke the clasp of hands near the exit, and ran. But the hijras are strong and don't give up. They lifted their sarees and followed me down the narrow wooden staircase. One grabbed my shirt and tore it. Others threw slippers at me. I ran fast shirtless, in track pants and pumps, hair flying in the breeze, through the tiny, winding streets, got lost in the thick human traffic, managed to regroup, jumped into a parked cab and told the cabbie to drive me wherever he wanted to, as long as it wasn't another brothel in the vicinity.

By now, I was getting used to a life on the run.

Writing on the red-light areas is difficult. But buttonholing the hijras is near impossible. They are intelligent, educated, widely travelled, articulate, strong and united. Whatever the odds, they stick together. They share their earnings, and there is great camaraderie among them. They also, strangely, boast a refined, elitist clientele.

Soon after the serial bomb blasts in Mumbai in 1993, which took a heavy toll of life and scarred the city for ever, I was assisting a colleague in a well-known foreign media network prepare a series of radio programmes on the city. The hijras are a good story for an international broadcast and so we did the customary reconnaissance of the hijra dens to get a feel of their circumstances. I knew their lives but my colleague needed to be convinced. She lived in London and was new to the violence of the lives of those occupying Mumbai's streets.

We decided to get them under one roof instead of ferreting them out from all over the city. That would have taken time and might not have resulted in much. So we got in touch with one of the leading NGOs working with the hijras and decided to meet at its office in central Mumbai, not far from the hijra homes.

The interview was going well. There were about forty hijras in the room. Even the seniors had come to air their views. This was important for the programme and we were lucky. The hijras have a strict hierarchy and the seniors are treated with reverence by the newcomers to the fold. They decide the agenda, and no one dare contest their words. Then my friend asked a question patently misplaced considering the peculiar circumstances we were in. She wasn't used to the nuances of the street in the subcontinent and let slip a costly error. 'God made man and God made woman,' she asked innocently without batting an eyelid as though she were covering the inauguration of an uptown beauty parlour. 'Why do you think He made you?' The moment the question slipped out of her there was silence in the room. The social workers of the

NGO and I exchanged glances. We tried to intervene and distract the pregnant moment from further attention. But the hijras had heard the words clearly and wouldn't let go.

'What do you mean?' growled the seniormost hijra after a pause, nearly tearing my eardrums. 'Do you think you are superior to us?' She then delivered a fiery speech that galvanized the others into action. They pounced on both of us, destroyed the tapes, the cameras and the recording equipment.

The senior hijra then lifted her saree, caught my bewildered friend's head in her large hands and thrust it deep into her naked genitals. 'See what God made,' she screamed. She held the head there for close to ten long, agonizing minutes. She later walked up to me and caught me in a tight grip like a sumo wrestler. I almost died of suffocation. She was taller than me and double my size. I just stood still. I couldn't even pray. I was used to such clutches in the suburban train but this had a sharp edge of uncertainty to it. After a few minutes, she let go but continued with her vituperation. The entire office was ransacked and the hijras left in a huff.

My colleague broke down. She collapsed in a heap, recovered hours later, and left Mumbai the same evening, never to return.

Cities change a lot, but red-light areas are old and change little. Take Delhi. It is also a city that doesn't go out of its way to respect women. No doors are opened for the fairer sex. Rape, molestation and murder happen all the time. Women are felt all over in buses and public spaces, they are ogled all the time, and are easy targets if alone. Even women with male companions have been attacked, and as I write this gang rape in moving cars is getting to be fashionable in the capital. A woman is picked up from the road, repeatedly raped in the car that continues to negotiate traffic, and then dumped like an old gunny bag in some quiet corner of the city. The police are busy looking after the politician and the force is stretched thin like a rubber band about to snap. Justice will invariably be delayed.

Delhi is also a city of migrants and is a pit stop for new money. Social inequities have risen dramatically over the years. The beautiful people have their private entertainment parlours, and the poor migrant has G.B. Road, which also doubles up as Swami Shradhanand Marg in a quixotic display of schizophrenia that has afflicted the road-naming authority.

It is a long and busy road like any other in India, without any remarkably distinguishing features. The ground floors are littered with shops, and there is the noise and energy of ritual shopping. But, whatever the season, come nightfall and the upper floors wake up to song, dance, merriment and the luscious tousle of female flesh on sale. G.B. Road is as dangerous as the streets of Delhi. Only here, the tables are turned. It is the men who are attacked.

On my reporting odysseys in the late 1980s, I made it a point to visit G.B. Road only with friends. There is safety in numbers here. If you are alone, you are drugged, beaten up and stripped of all belongings. If you wake up from the assault, you will need weeks of intensive care followed by months of overtime at the office to make up for the losses. So, covering the goings-on is difficult. Any perceived discourtesy, however slight, is given the treatment. You have to be polite, quick and be ready to part with cash at the slightest signs of disapproval. I learnt the tricks the hard way. The unfriendliness of G.B. Road has also contributed to the flourishing call girl trade in the capital and the birth of several new centres of customer-friendly sexual opportunity.

Chennai in the south is a different cup of steaming tea. It is where I studied and grew up. It is where I return to recharge, to gaze endlessly at the water buffaloes, large and black and seemingly without care, and join the rush on the East Coast Road to Puducherry or opt for other adventures that beckon the wanderer at every bend in the road.

The old bastion of flesh trade is a nondescript neighbourhood called Koddambakkam. It is dotted with small independent dwellings and slum colonies. Kodambakkam also headquarters the Tamil film industry. Nothing in Chennai is brazenly displayed. Even the wealthy seem somewhat wary of ostentatious displays of money. It may have something to do with the powerful hold of orthodoxy on the city. As a result, prostitution, though well and alive, is buried deep, unlike in Mumbai where it is thrown at your face. You have to recruit the middleman for help. He could be a professional pimp or a taxi or auto driver.

Chennai has a perennial water shortage, a merciless sun beating down on it even in the winter, and demonic walls of hypocrisy growing more gigantic by the day. Single women in trendy clothes avoid the poorly lit streets after sunset. Nearly all watering holes and public spaces are crowded out by men. Large curtains of morality are indiscriminately thrown around. Organized prostitution is the first casualty in this massive crackdown on sex, love and freedom of choice.

Of course, thanks to all the policing, the flesh trade is flourishing with a vengeance. On one of my visits, the young tout who agreed to be my guide, mistook me for a policeman in disguise until he warmed up to my silly jokes. Till then, our excursions bordered on the ridiculous. When I asked him to take me to a cabaret, he took me to a large dimly-lit hall off Anna Salai, the city's largest artery. For an exorbitant fee, scores of men had gathered around tables to watch women dance. The women were expectedly heaving away but were completely covered. All that the male gaze could see were naked dark feet and silver toe rings that occasionally reflected the dim lights. The alcohol served cost three times the retail price, and more adventure cost a fortune. It was then that the tout, for some strange reason, probably because I had bought him a drink, realized that I wasn't a government informer. He relaxed a bit, said a hundred 'sawrrees', and confessed that since he was now certain that I wouldn't book him under any law, he would show me the heart of the business. I was touched. 'But it is very expensive, saar,' he admitted, now clearly on my side. I bought him another drink and ensured complete loyalty from him for the next six months. The sex trade evidently had acquired a new black market.

One incident, though, is not easy to let go. A colleague and I (we were both reporting HIV/AIDS in India and the only way to get the real story is to plunge into the hot spots disguised as customers) visited one of the more hyped-up brothels in one of the better localities of the city. It was a large bungalow built on three levels in a shady side street. As we approached it one solemn evening, a man emerged from the shadows and asked us if he was right in guessing why we had come.

Everyone in Chennai is polite and respectful and he was no exception. We congratulated him on this excellent piece of detection. He then told us to wait and disappeared into the same shadows that he had emerged from. He returned after a few minutes with another man. We followed them for a while and were motioned to stop and park the car at a secluded spot. We were then led on foot until a small door surreptitiously opened for us to enter. It was still very dark and we could barely make out silhouettes.

The bungalow was teeming with men. Valet parking was available and cars were parked all along the adjoining streets. We met the madam, who smiled and told us that there were only three girls available and that they had come from Bangalore and were heavily booked. She told us that it could be a few hours' wait and that we could make ourselves comfortable in the visitor's room.

To amuse us, she presented us an album of the girls naked. There were also photographs of them copulating with different men.

We thanked her for her hospitality and fixed an appointment for the next evening when the girls would finally be through with their exertions and would hopefully have time for us. In turn, she thanked us in excellent English for taking the trouble of supporting her business and asked one of the hangers-on to take us safely back to the car. We were ceremonially escorted on the return journey. We gave the man ten rupees and he saluted smartly.

Nothing on the street beat has been more strange.

I have briefly touched on the four largest Indian cities. A more detailed coverage will run into several riveting volumes. But what is important here is that the spread of the HIV is everywhere. The northeast is battling intravenous drug use and the virus has reached the villages and smaller towns of India as migratory multitudes look for deliverance from their parched lands.

Every step of my travels through the length and breadth of India celebrated excitement; from rickshaw-pullers in Rajasthan who believed that the German women they married were white goddesses who fell from the sky to Arabs in Mumbai brothels looking for virgins to cure them of venereal disease. In truth, the German women were smuggling drugs across the border into India and had used the men to extend their stay, and the Arabs were being waylaid by the hard sell of glib street charlatans and a tireless libido seeking new ways to express itself. Then there were the stark contradictions: entire communities selling sex for a livelihood and others for whom celibacy was a way of life. And, running through it all, like a crooked vertebrae, was promiscuity and perversion.

But let's look at the bright side. For the first time, over a billion people knew what a condom was even if they couldn't spell or pronounce it right. It took a killer virus to introduce them to what the family planning czars had failed to do for so many decades.

India is strewn with so many diverse and incomprehensible cultural contexts and subtexts. Covering a sensitive topic like sexuality and a disease that emanates from it in a land that still practises secret and unsafe sex is a challenge. Where do you draw the line and whom do you include? At one level India is brazenly promiscuous, at another level it is scared to even mention the word. Between the two extremes are innumerable zones of contention. Covering it all has been an exhilarating experience. I have been threatened with knives, hit, kicked and verbally abused. If I hadn't honed my survival skills and been a good runner, I would have been dead by now. A sense of humour, which acquired a new dimension along the way, also helped.

CHAPTER 9

STREET VOICES

No one means all he says, and yet very few say all they mean, for words are slippery and thought is viscous.

— Henry Brooks Adams

I have lived on Mumbai's streets and seen its moods up close. Its bleeding colours are appealing to the excitement junkie. But you have to visit it at your leisure and not be sentenced to it. Otherwise you are dead meat. Interestingly, I have also had visitors from the Western world who insisted on booking into a street instead of a hotel room! It was much cheaper and they got to see India with different eyes. They would take a taxi from the airport and settle on a pavement of their choice. They travelled light; a large sleeping bag with several pockets for immediate needs was sufficient. They also knew that if they were willing to spend money they would get whatever they needed, including police protection. They just loved it.

Every year, they would leave their homes for two months in the winter and land on the streets of Mumbai. They would smoke hashish, make girlfriends, sometimes babies too; a few even married those they consorted with on the streets. Some studied the city as sociologists; there were writers, painters and artists who looked at the street for inspiration. They took photographs, parted with cash for conveniences, and when there was just enough money remaining for the taxi ride back to the airport, they would have a haircut and shave and slip into the role of the air traveller. Several others wormed their way into the bowels of the city and made profitable contacts. It is easy to get lost in Mumbai. You can slip into any fold and there is so much happening all the time that it takes inordinate tenacity to ferret you out. The cops, even if they mean well, have other demands on their time.

In all fairness, the street allows a poor person to live reasonably well when compared to what he has left behind in his village. Sundry jobs are always available in every fissure of the city. At least food, clothing, a livelihood and some fun can always be had. Since you are always on the fringes of the law, might is right. The rules of the street are primitive. Only the fittest survive. If you have your wits around you and biceps that flex with gusto, the helpless ones seek you out. Make the right connections and you go places. If you don't, you still mange a job, some food and entertainment. You still manage to live.

Music is essentially useless, as life is: but both have an ideal extension which lends utility to its conditions.

—George Santayana

Madiya is ten years old. He is short and dark with untidy hair that is matted and dry. He has his name tattooed in Hindi on the inside of his right arm. A cheap, glistening bracelet adorns his left wrist. He has a sweet, little-boy-lost-in-the-woods look and an intelligent gleam in his eyes.

We meet on the street. He is playing a rustic homemade violin with some expertise outside Churchgate station and the crowds are on tiptoe, straining heads and shoulders to catch a glimpse of the source of this wonderful Hindi film music. Churchgate station is packed all day and night as trains load and unload large numbers of people without letting up. There is no time to waste. Ask any Mumbaikar, even the poorest, and he will tell you that time is money. Yet, Madiya manages to distract them.

I whisk him away to an Irani restaurant near the railway tracks and we talk about his life over milk tea and bun-maska (bread and butter). 'I am from Rajasthan,' he tells me with the air of one who is proud to buy his own meal. 'From a family of musicians. We came to Mumbai two years ago to earn a livelihood. We live on the pavement in Khar but I leave early and return late. I am the eldest. There are my parents, two brothers and four sisters. One brother ran away from home. My father hit him when he was drunk. He ran away in fear.'

Madiya's father gave him the violin and taught him to play it. 'It is easy,' he tells me. 'As far as I can remember, the first thing that I ever held was a violin. I just fiddled with it. Then I learnt the tunes. I can now play the latest film songs in Hindi, Marathi and Gujarati as well as many folk songs from my hometown.'

Madiya travels all over Mumbai and plays wherever he instinctively feels he can make some money. He makes a few hundred rupees on a good day, but there are bad days too. If he is lucky and bumps into a group of foreigners, he makes enough money to last months. 'They give me a lot of money in foreign currency,' he says innocently. 'The foreigners love my tunes and ask me to play them again and again. They even ask me to come to their country but I don't want to leave my people. I will be so lonely.' He gives his mother whatever he earns because she prepares food for him and gets him new clothes while his father spends the money on drink and beats up the entire family. 'If he knows I have money, he will beat me too,' he says simply.

Madiya belongs to a tribe of musicians from Jawalbandha in Rajasthan. They are nomadic and travel all the time looking for places where more money can be earned. Wherever they are, they return home every Diwali and celebrate with song and drink. And then begins, once again, the long journey to the big cities of India for food.

'Mumbai is different from home. I don't like it. The police harass us all the time. They jailed me the other day and let me go only after my parents came to fetch me. Nobody troubles us in our village. We are free to do whatever we please. If we see the police here we have to run or they take all our money, beat us up and jail us.'

Madiya's parents are a performing duo. His father plays the violin and his mother sings. The family spreads out to different parts of the city in the morning and meets up at night to determine how much there is in the kitty. Then the earnings are divided based on seniority and need. His mother needs a bit more for the provisions and his father for his drink.

'I don't smoke or drink like the other boys my age,' says Madiya. 'I don't even see films. Most of the time there isn't enough to eat. When I grow up I want to go back to my village and work on the land. If I continue here, I will have to spend the rest of my life singing for a meal. It makes hunger more painful.'

There are many ways of breaking a heart. Stories were full of hearts broken by love, but what really broke a heart was taking away its dream – whatever that dream might be.
—Pearl S. Buck

'I am from Nashik,' he tells me. We are on Juhu beach and it is raining heavily. It has been raining like this for days. The seafront is littered with plastic, some lovers are smooching away on the beach under raincoats, and even the stray dogs that loiter around have decided against romping on the beach. The cops, too, are staying away.

The sea is snarling ferociously. I have an umbrella to protect myself, but the rain is pouring down Ramu's torn T-shirt and shorts. 'My father died four years ago and mother left the family soon after,' he says. 'I am the eldest of five brothers.' The wind and the waves are shrieking and rivulets of water are gathering the beach sand in folds. It's dark, late and wet. There is not a soul in sight, barring the lovers, on the vast arc of the lonely beach.

'This is Gangaram,' he says, pointing to the monkey. Ramu holds Gangaram by a leash, but it is more out of habit than to control the monkey's movements. Gangaram looks at him with love and some pride. They need one another; it is a difficult bond to decipher. Like most relationships that hover deliriously on irrational attachment, it will, in all likelihood, leave the other shattered in an anticlimactic end. They are treading the tightrope, dangerously balancing the other. But I can see the attachment that lives in their eyes. There is sorrow, loneliness and longing in every tug, every pull. They know what the other needs instinctively. In this wide world with its opulence and penury, faith and hopelessness, birth, love and death, Ramu and Gangaram have only one another, and even that togetherness has been roped in by several strange circumstances.

Suddenly, in the midst of our conversation, Gangaram jumps on to Ramu and tries to hide under his wet T-shirt. Scared, he holds him hard. On this vast stretch of sand, overseen by the bungalows of the rich and the shimmer of hazy city lights in the distance, with the sea and the rain tearing away at anything that will cramp their style, a monkey and a man settle for an embrace.

I can see the love in Gangaram's eyes. He wipes the rain from Ramu's face, pulls his nose and playfully bites him on the cheek. Ramu appears annoyed and smacks him a trifle hard. Gangaram jumps and sits on Ramu's head and plucks away at the follicles. The rain has subsided a bit, and we talk with the wet earth sinking beneath our feet.

'I have been living off Gangaram for the last four years,' says Ramu. 'From the money I earn I not only look after the two of us but the rest of the family too.' The family consists of four younger brothers. They stay on the pavement in Andheri, a Mumbai suburb. Ramu was gifted Gangaram by his uncle when the monkey was a few months old. 'He is very intelligent,' continues Ramu. 'He learnt all my tricks in a few weeks. He can jump, roll, play dead and do all the acrobatics. He is also very mischievous. He does salaam, collects the money and doesn't want to give it to me. He can even walk like a policeman. Look, I will show you.' He gives Gangaram a command and the monkey walks erect and arrogant, a stick rolled between his hands, looking at all life around him with disdain.

Ramu had two monkeys before getting Gangaram. But they were fatally struck by a mysterious fever during the monsoon many years ago. 'I still remember the day,' he says. 'It was one of the most tragic days of my life.' Monkeys are easily available in Mumbai. A little one, barely a few weeks old, can be bought for less than a thousand rupees. Nomadic tribes wander around India with their children, their monkeys and several heads of cattle. The monkeys are well-trained and well taken care of and they all live together like a large joint family, even eating out of the same plate. They are also paired for life.

Ramu makes about two hundred rupees a day. 'But it all depends,' he says. 'Today, I haven't eaten anything and I have to feed Gangaram. He loves bananas and when I can afford it, I give him bread and chapattis and a little milk. He eats what we eat, even rice and curry. I feel sad when I can't feed him enough.'

Ramu is nineteen and has never been to school. None of his brothers has been to school either. 'If I had some education I wouldn't be doing this,' he says. 'It's like begging,' he says. 'The struggle is to eat. Everything comes after that. I have no other distractions. Sometimes I see a film during the festival season when it is free. When I am tired, I have a paan or a beedi. I don't drink or smoke ganja like so many others on the beach.'

Ramu comes to Juhu beach with Gangaram every day at eight in the morning and stays on till the late hours of the night. Gangaram jumps and somersaults for all he is worth and they return to the pavement in Andheri and feed themselves and the others at home with the pickings of the day.

'I have no friends,' he says. 'At times I feel really lonely. It is a shattering thought. I think it will be nice to have a wife who can share my pain and understand what I am going through.' A girl has been chosen for him in the village, but he needs at least five thousand rupees to get married. He doesn't have the money and will have to wait till he collects the amount.

'I like Mumbai,' he says. Then he thinks for a while, and adds, 'Actually it doesn't matter where you are. When you don't have money in the pocket and food in your belly, nothing matters.'

The rain has petered to a halt, and the sea breathes easy.

Work out your own salvation. Do not depend on others.
—Buddha

In Kala Ghoda, opposite the Jehangir Art Gallery, a middle-aged woman in a cheap, moth-eaten polyester saree draws lustily on the dying end of her beedi. Leaning against a lamppost, she gives every passer-by the glad eye, showing off a cleavage soaked in powder and sweat. Next to her, urchins are huddled together greedily preparing a round of smack. Along with the whore and the junkie, the castaways of society somehow land up on Hope Street. Yes, that's what the street is called!

But hope is at hand. All is not lost. Swami Sadanand Saraswati, the resident soothsayer, is a few feet away. He looks as imposing as his name. His short, frail body is covered in thin white cotton that could do with a run at the cleaners. A badly grown ponytail, a matted goatee, sandalwood streaks on his forehead, arms and chest, a six-mukhi rudraksha bead string around the neck and horn-rimmed spectacles complete a picture of silent erudition.

The swami is an engaging fellow. He bursts into Sanskrit whenever caught unprepared, laughs easily, and has eyes that pop out like a stethoscope and search your soul. Add a glib tongue to it all and he is a huge success. He has been on the street for close to three decades.

Thousands of men and women have come to him over the years with their tears, joys, longings and apprehensions. He has mastered the art of reading the body and the mind. One look with his loud eyes and he knows what to say. For effect, he picks out a magnifying glass from his bag and scours both palms. Then he rattles off with the bad news first. The good news is reserved for the end like a little bribe to placate your soul. No punches are held back.

He says it straight and true. He offers palliatives in the form of lucky gems and prayers on auspicious days. He also throws up ayurvedic remedies for simple ailments. Customers have returned to him for more along with friends and family. Everyone consults him: lawyers, policemen, journalists, students, bureaucrats, businessmen and even the local sex worker. Love, money and health are the common concerns. Swamiji is friend to all, an institution on the street.

'I was born in Tanjore in the south of India,' he tells me. I am seated with him on the pavement and we order chai. He also tells me my future and keeps rattling off the milestones in my life before I change tack and insist that he talk about his life.

He studied a bit and then his father died while he was still very young. Without the money to study further, he left home when he was eleven years old and went to Chennai, the big city close by. 'It was a tough time,' he continues. 'I didn't know what to do. I joined up with a political party, which was easy, anyone can join up, but it was not what I really wanted to do. I soon got fed up of the processions and 'dharnas' and went to Benaras. I wandered around and returned to Chennai a broken man. I had no money, no real education and no survival skills. I sat in a temple and cried. I thought it was the end for me. The temple priest took pity on me. He introduced me to an ayurvedic practitioner who was also a holy man. He took care of me and taught me. He fed me, gave me a place to stay and looked after me like his own son. That's when my life turned on its head.'

Swamiji studied ayurveda, the Vedas, Sanskrit, astrology, numerology and religion. Suitably nourished with food and education, he travelled all over India 'to see how people lived in different parts of the country' and then landed in Mumbai where he has remained ever since. He found a home in the suburbs and a spot on the pavement in the heart of town, and soon realized that his knowledge and erudition would help fill his stomach. He became an instant hit. People flocked to him for advice. He charges very little even to this day. If a customer says he doesn't have the money, the Swami lets him go with his blessings. 'I am not crazy about money. I want to serve people, that's all,' he says.

Swamiji checks the horoscope, too, but says he has 'full faith in palmistry. It is 80 per cent correct. The lines on the finger are the most reliable. They don't change much. I can read a person like a book. I have even predicted death. I believe in karma and destiny. Not too much that has been ordained can be changed. But if I feel that a person is not psychologically equipped to handle dire predictions, I just mildly hint at tough times ahead and how to deal with it. I tell the person to pray. After all, I am not God, and prayer and good acts can also change one's destiny.'

Swamiji is well organized. His mind is razor sharp. Though he doesn't write anything down, he remembers customers, their birth details and earlier predictions. 'When people don't tell me much, I read their faces and startle them. But I try not to look at more than ten palms a day. It gets tiring. All types of people come for consultation and many have negative energies. I don't encourage them. It gets very draining. I have also forecast my own life and it has been accurate so far. I know when I will die.'

The good man also dispenses ayurvedic medicines and advises people on how to control their minds and optimize their lives. He is now married to a woman twenty-five years younger and has four children. 'I had predicted my mother's death too at the age of eighty-two. Mankind must live in love. That is the only salvation,' is his parting shot. He also tells me that India's future is great!

I took a speed reading course and read 'War and Peace' in twenty minutes. It involves Russia.

—Woody Allen

Lalji Kamtaprasad Pande is a giant of a man. Over six feet tall and powerfully built, he missed out on a career in freestyle wrestling by the vagaries of circumstance. Another place, another time and he would have been a winner in a different ring. Today, he sells books and magazines on the pavement outside Churchgate station, something he has been doing for over sixty years. He is no marketing guru but Pande knows what sells on the street like no other. He has seen the British go and several governments fall. In his eighties now, he knows that the business is well tended to by his sons and that there is not much time left for him on this earth. He is taking it easy. Which means he just won't stop talking.

'I am from Jaunpur zilla near Allahabad,' he says. 'I came to Mumbai in search of a livelihood. My elder brother was already here selling magazines. So I did the easiest thing. I joined him. I didn't have to struggle.'

Pande has been witness to the meteoric growth of Indian journalism. When he began, Indian papers were printed on letterpress and then offset. There was no television in India and computers were unheard of. It was a different world. He tells me about the leading papers and magazines and the number of copies he sold everyday. Most of them don't exist now. But today's India is not the India Pande is in touch with and he faintly recognizes that truth.

Even to this day he wakes up at five in the morning. He used to stay on the pavement but hard work gave him the money to get himself a roof over his head. His three sons run the show but he insists on overseeing the work, which continues till midnight. He tells me that he studied only till the eighth standard but he 'read all the papers and magazines he sold and learnt everything'. He has his take on every aspect of Indian life: from politics to pornography. 'The British were very good,' he says. 'Pandit Nehru, Indira and Rajiv also did a lot. The others are rascals and looted the country. Everyone is looting India today. The rupee has no value now. Everything has gone out of control. There is no purity or truth. The world is coming to an end.'

I ask him the secret of his robust health. It will take a few good men to knock him down even today. 'I don't smoke or drink or watch films. I eat very little. All that I like to do is to go to the races. There is no money for other things. Those days the air was clean. Food and water was excellent. We worked hard all the time. There was no corruption. Look at my sons. They don't have my strength because they have been brought up in Mumbai. I grew up in the village and in the fields where the air is still so pure. We have some land back home but it is not enough to support all of us. There is no money to live. So we have to be here in Mumbai. But my shop is special. Big shots come here, all educated and learned. People who read books and magazines are special people. You see, this is not a bhelpuri shop.'

In the middle of difficulty lies opportunity.
                                                    —Albert Einstein

Colaba has a slew of eateries. Bagdadi behind the Taj Mahal Palace Hotel is a legend. Nearly everyone who has passed through Mumbai has eaten there at least once. The food is tasty, cheap and the service fast. It is a functional place. You go there to eat and not to serenade your woman. There are tables and chairs, a large jug of water and loads of sliced white onion and lemon in little saucers to accompany the meal.

The portions are huge and Bagdadi's reputation has spilled through the *Lonely Planet* to every corner of the world. His clientele is international. Bagdadi's best advertisement was the Pakistani hockey team, which used to eat there when it was in Mumbai for the World Cup. When they couldn't visit, the food was delivered to the five-star hotel that accommodated them. For the everyday customer, it's a delight. It's quality food at reasonable rates. You walk in, eat and walk out. That's it. Maybe, add a belch to the pattern. The only catch is that once you are in, you are hooked. You just have to return for another meal.

The cooks at Bagdadi have remained for years, ensuring quality, but the waiters come and go. They come from different parts of India, get a job to keep going, sight greener pastures and then move on. Colaba is a huge tourist destination with an array of distractions. If you are lucky, your dreams can work out. If you are not so careful and slip into the junkie-sex-worker trail, which is the easier option, your descent into the quicksand is nightmarish.

I know so many who died miserably of an overdose of sex and heroin. I also know several who came to the streets with nothing, hooked up with a backpacker or found a job overseas and never returned to India. If they ever did, it was as a rich tourist to meet up with old friends and check out the seedy lanes whose womb they once filled with their dreams. Call it destiny or intelligence, but the line is wafer thin. I would root for destiny because a homeless teenager is ruled more by the hormone rush than a sense of planning. When the senses can get pleasured so easily and in such bounty, it is difficult to think straight. So those who were delivered from the nightmare were just lucky.

Raju came to Mumbai from Kolkata seeking his pot of gold. In his twenties, tall, dusky and thin, he has an endearing smile and eyes that accompany it. He got a job in Bagdadi as a waiter and that's how we met. I used to eat there frequently when I first came to Mumbai. In fifteen rupees, I could manage a big meal and a bigger belch. With a little more I could even have a birthday party.

'I am from Kidderpore in Kolkata,' he says, starting his story. 'I came to this city fascinated by the glamour and to expand my horizons. I got a job easily. I just walked in here and got the job. They pay me a little, give me food and allow me to stay here. Once a year, the management presents all of us with a new pant and shirt. I get a lot of tips too and can even send money back home. It's a good deal. I am lucky.' Raju is the eldest in the family. His father retired from a lifetime with the Indian Railways. 'Now that I am here, there is no going back. The city is exciting. Colaba is mindblowing. I would like to settle down in Mumbai or get out of India. But no going back to Kolkata. It is a dead city.'

Raju is very likeable. He is the most popular waiter. He never loses his cool and is forever smiling. He can also be trusted. He wears the aura of trust easily. 'Foreigners are very fond of me. A French couple invited me to France but I didn't go. They have called me again. I don't know what to do. Should I go?' Raju hasn't gone to school but speaks several languages fluently. He picked them up on the job while serving a multiracial clientele. 'I read the dictionary every night, read books and watch television. I like to meet different kinds of people. I am learning all the time. I haven't been to school. So this is the best way to learn.'

I met Raju over several months and he was evolving fast. The little lad from Kolkata had fitted in nicely in the most happening locality of glamorous Mumbai. Now he was keen on spreading his wings. 'Colaba is fascinating. It's like the whole world has been reduced to one locality. But now I am thinking of going abroad. Anywhere. I have job offers from the Gulf and have been invited to France and England by my clients. They have promised to help me.' A year later, he came to bid me goodbye. 'I have got a job in Saudi Arabia. Before taking it up I am going to France for a holiday. I also think I like a French girl,' he said shyly. 'I am going with her.'

Welcome to Mumbai, the city of dreams.

O, it is excellent to have a giant's strength; but it is tyrannous to use it like a giant.
—William Shakespeare, *Measure for Measure*

Like creepers growing out of crags, they trail the railway tracks at Jogeshwari, a Mumbai suburb. They have settled on the space around the railway line, but they won't be there for long. They are nomads, forever on the move.

It is a hot afternoon. The sun is baking my face. I walk into the settlement and see hundreds of them in the comfort of domesticity. They are a beautiful race. Dark, adorned with trinkets and well built. They look like they have hopped out of a time machine for a break. I just stand and stare.

There are hordes of naked children playing with dogs, cats, monkeys, large black lizards with darting tongues, and pigs. The nomads carry their animals with them wherever they go. Little children tear at their mother's swollen, black teats, the men are erecting tents and the women are cooking. They could have escaped from a nudist camp, a *National Geographic* frame or a Spielberg set. No one wears anything really, in some cases not even the bare essentials.

Enormous breasts and gorgeous faces with tattoos turn around to face me, and I don't mind that, but when the men and the dogs notice me I decide that it may not be a good idea to keep staring, and move on. I am in jeans, a full-sleeved shirt and pumps. I am an alien for them.

In certain sections of India, scantily-clad men and women hog celebrity status. Their only claim to fame is a lack of inhibition. If you can parade naked, drink a bit at parties and lock lips in full view, all sorts of talent gets added to your persona and you are marketed as an icon for Generation Next. These are people who can afford clothing – it is their nakedness that is being celebrated.

India lives in so many zones that the mind just boggles. Which is the real India? Where does it live? How can such diverse peoples ever see eye to eye under a tricolour?

I keep walking, pretending that I haven't seen anything. A few yards away, rapid construction activity is crucifying open land. After that is a barren stretch. Parched and broken by fissures. In the only green patch visible, so out of place in the brown dustiness, is Ziarath Ali. Built like a heritage steam engine with a golden beard on his wrinkled, parchment-like expressive face, he is the watchman of the area. He has been on the job for over fifty years.

For one, who could well be a chronicler of life considering his age and time spent on the job, Ali doesn't talk much. He labours with answers, hides facts, gets irritated easily, and sticks to precise answers. He isn't unfriendly. It's just the way he is. While we talk, he cleans his hands with petrol.

Ali was born in Peshawar in Pakistan. He left home before India and Pakistan were made two countries in 1947 and came to Mumbai looking for work. He had no education and was very poor. But he is almost seven feet tall and well over 300 pounds. As a young man, sheer muscle would have opened doors. If they didn't, he could have broken them down.

'This place was a jungle,' he explains. 'I supervised the grass cutting. The grass grew till my shoulders. It was my job to keep the place clean and prevent animals and human beings from entering this space. I am doing the same job today. But it is all so different now. Those days there was nothing here for miles on end. It was a thick jungle. There were wild animals. Robbers used to come here. They saw me and ran away. No one dares challenge Ali.'

He continues, 'Land was in plenty. The owner of this plot was a lonely man. He had no family. He liked me and told me to take as much land as I wanted. He used to sit and drink. But I refused. What would I do with all this land? I had no ambitions. But I didn't know then that people would spend so much money one day to buy land here. Today, this land is so expensive. But I have no need for it.'

Ali has a small kitchen garden and cooks his meals in a little hut close by. He has also dug a well all by himself. 'Anyone can take my vegetables and my water. After all, God has given it.' I ask him about his size. 'Yes, people look at me and get frightened. I am a Pathan. It takes at least ten men to kill a Pathan,' he says, proudly straightening his back and thumping his chest like Tarzan. I am not particularly small but I notice that I am the size of his right arm.

'We are the strongest and bravest in the world. If you come to Peshawar we are all like this. I used to eat two kilos of raw meat straight from the butcher as a young man. I would tear it with my hands and gobble it. I used to eat raw fish too. Grab the fish from the river and just eat it raw. No vegetables or anything.'

Ali has never been to school and says he remembers nothing about his childhood. He doesn't travel either. He hasn't even seen the rest of the city. He doesn't leave the plot of land entrusted to his care even for a day. He married twice and has great-grandchildren. 'I don't know much. I don't talk to others. You keep asking me questions and so I answer. I don't care about you. My job is to keep this place safe and clean and I will do it till I die. I have a hut to sleep in and food to eat. Now I don't eat so much. I don't need anything else. Okay, I have to go on my rounds. If there is anything else you want to know, come tomorrow at the same time.'

He hitches his coloured lungi around his waist, puffs up his chest that is larger than his vegetable patch and walks off.

1. At the rise of the hand of the policeman, stop rapidly. Do not pass him or otherwise disrespect him.
2. If pedestrian obstacle your path, tootle horn melodiously. If he continues to obstacle, tootle horn vigorously and utter vocal warning as 'Hi,Hi...'
5. Beware of greasy corner where lurk skid demon. Cease step on, approach slowly, round cautiously, resume step on gradually.

—from an official Japanese guide for
English-speaking drivers, 1936

Cynicism came early in life to Denis Michael Lewis, even before he began viewing life through the windscreen and the rearview mirror of his Fiat taxi. Mumbai has close to 70,000 taxis. They are available any time of the day or night. They run on metres and the driver has a white card with the rates printed on them in red. Owners who drive their taxis are normally in white shirts and pants and those who have rented them are in brown shirts and pants. It is a demarcation insisted on by the vigilant traffic police, who also have a legendary lease on notoriety.

Most taxis are clean and well-maintained and the service is very professional, easily the best in India. There are no arguments over the fare and the drivers are generally well-behaved and law-abiding. The fares increase substantially if the taxi is hailed after midnight and then reverts to the normal rate around daybreak. The latest models are now being incorporated into the fleet. Several are air-conditioned and all the new cars are environment- and cost-friendly. However, before they take over the streets completely, they will have to ride the wave of protesting taxi unions.

Many drivers live in their taxis. It is more convenient than going home. In a city teeming with people, they are always on call. Driving around in Mumbai is uncomfortable and parking is difficult. So the taxi is in great demand even among those who own cars. Most of the taxi drivers in Mumbai are from other parts of India. The majority is from Uttar Pradesh, a state with more people than Germany and the United Kingdom together. In a city that lives on the edge, the taxi driver invariably grows large eyes and ears. He plays several roles. Being the driver is just one of them. He could also be a part of the mafia, a police informer or even a sex-crazed maniac living vicariously through the rear-view mirror. He could also interchange roles and play all of them simultaneously when he feels like it. I have met several taxi drivers who knew more about the city than all the mayors put together. They could provide any news channel the biggest scoop ever, but they are also smart enough to value their lives and know when to keep their mouths tightly shut. It takes nothing to extinguish life in Mumbai. Another murder will happen in no time and the previous one ejected from memory like a slice of burnt bread from a toaster. And who wants to die? The taxi driver is truly the smartest man on Mumbai's streets. He sees it all but still knows nothing!

Denis Michael, from Mangalore, is different. All that he wants is to make a living and look after his wife and three daughters. He is religious and goes to church every Sunday. He lives off the earnings from his taxi and if he is not comfortable with the customer who has hailed his cab, he will refuse the fare. 'I don't want trouble,' he says. 'Jesus is always watching.' A cross on his chest is also watching over him.

Denis is in his fifties. He is also the owner of the taxi. 'I like the feeling of independence. I had taken a bank loan and paid off the money. Now I am free. I don't have to listen to someone I don't like. When I want to drive, I drive. When I don't want to, I stay at home.'

Denis is well dressed; his cab owner's white uniform is washed and ironed and has no fraying edges. To prevent the sweat and grime of a humid city from getting to his crisp shirt collar, he has placed a large, brown handkerchief around his neck. His polished badge is displayed on the left pocket of his shirt. Clean shaven, hair cut short with a side parting, he has a little, neat, dyed moustache. Denis seems particular about the little things in life.

His taxi is also well maintained. It has a fresh coat of paint and the interiors are done up with plastic flowers and colourful little bulbs which give the cab a happy feel. A statue of Mother Mary is placed near the steering wheel. He keeps cleaning it with a yellow cloth that is now fading. The cushions are dark blue, lush and comfortable.

Getting around in Denis's taxi is quite a luxurious affair. He drives slowly and observes all the traffic rules. He doesn't smoke, doesn't chew paan and so doesn't spit it out of the window on unsuspecting passers-by like the others, and doesn't use cuss words. I have used taxis for years and met drivers who could make Bud Spencer look like Mother Teresa at prayer time, but Denis is the gentlest, most well mannered and affable taxi driver I have ever met. He almost seems frightened to drive on Mumbai streets.

'My wife is a nurse,' he continues, happy to talk to me. 'Everything is expensive and so it is important for husband and wife to earn. I will educate my daughters and send them abroad. There is a great demand for nurses in other countries. Let them earn well and make their lives. I have my own place here. After they are settled, I will go back to Mangalore and live peacefully. My wife has lot of property. I left Mumbai many times. Got fed

up driving this taxi. But got bored and came back. There is life in
Mumbai. Mangalore is boring. There is nothing to do. How long
can you look at the scenery? So I came back. I see everything that
is happening here. But I believe in Jesus and pray to him when I
am troubled. He helps me.'

I ask him about what he has seen that has been so disturbing.
'Everything,' he says. I prod him, and persist. 'What can I say? Now
don't get me into any trouble. I am not involved in anything. I am
a taxi driver, that's all. Please understand.' I assure him that there
won't be trouble. He tells me that he has driven taxis for thirty-
two years. 'In such a long time you see everything. You see guns,
bombs, everything. Sometimes, a boy and a girl take the taxi and
start making love. Once a couple undressed completely. I saw it
in the mirror. I have daughters. I stopped the taxi and told them
to dress up and go home. They offered me double. I told them
that I don't want any payment. I said that I would go to the police
and I would tell their parents. They got scared and ran away. This
happens all the time. People think the taxi is the bedroom. If they
don't have any place to go to, why don't they choose another taxi?
Prostitutes also bring their customers. It is cheaper in a taxi and
there are no raids. I don't like all this. Now please don't get me
into trouble.' I pat him on the back in gentle reassurance.

He then tells me about police harassment, about customers who
promise to pay and then vanish and how he has even been robbed
at knifepoint. 'All this happens in the night. But I don't go to the
red-light area and other dangerous spots and if I see a group that
is drunk I don't take them. They also take drugs in the taxi. They
stop it in a corner, all educated boys and girls from good families,
and take drugs. If we see a police van coming, they ask me to
drive. Sometimes, I have to do all this. They pay me well, much
more than the cab fare. If I say no to everything, I won't be able
to drive my taxi. I can't help it but I also overhear conversations
and I can tell you many things, but I won't. I have talked about

this to my wife. She says it is okay, that life is like this. She is a nurse in a municipal hospital. She also sees everything. I just pray to Jesus to forgive me.'

I can see that this conversation is disturbing Denis. He is on edge. So I suggest that we have a cup of tea and some biscuits. We drive to the entrance of the flesh district next door and park. Suddenly, there are gunshots and a mob is running towards us. There is blood all over. We duck for cover. The mob passes us and a police siren blares. Denis starts the cab and we take off. 'See, I told you what happens,' he says much later, still shaking, and trying to wipe the grime from the statute of Mother Mary looking at him without a change in expression.

When you have loved as she has loved, you grow old beautifully.
—W. Somerset Maugham

The Congress House, on the outer margins of the flesh district, is in the terminal stages of dilapidation. Like in the old chawls, tiny rooms open into a long corridor with a toilet at one end. The rooms are stark. There's a mattress, some pillows and a few clothes hanging from a string facing the window. Sunlight looks in and catches the clothes in its warmth.

There are a few buildings in a rectangular format, all embodying the final stages of life. The men sit on their haunches in old pyjamas and smoke bidis and have tea and the women cook. The lethargy is contagious. Mongrels laze in the sunlight sprawled on their backs looking up at the sky. The lice on them have also gone to sleep.

This is Congress House in the daytime.

Allow the afternoon sun to fall and the butterfly starts taking birth. The women bathe with care, dry their long, cascading hair without hurry and get down to the elaborate ritual of making themselves up. This can take hours. When the sun finally sets, they emerge as mannequins. They look so stunning in their rich Mughal finery that you feel that even the moon is making eyes at them when you are not watching. Every room is dazzling. The lights come on in chandeliers, music brings life to the ambience and the girls start dancing. Customers gather, money is thrown, more permanent relationships are discussed, and the night stretches a long, long way into daybreak.

Zeenat Begum is in charge of one of the rooms. She has seven girls singing for her. They vary in age from ten to thirty. They are as enchanting as one can dress the wildest fantasies in. Zeenat is in her early fifties and still lowers her eyes when your gaze tries to flatter them. She is fair, draped in jewellery and clad in flamboyant colours. She was a dancer once; now she teaches dance. Polite and elegant, she talks about her life.

Zeenat's mouth is stuffed with betel nut and as the night wears on she replaces it with imported whisky. Her feet are soft, tiny and pink, like a child's, and washed in olive oil. She has the nails painted in red. Her heels and soles are touched with henna. Barring her face and feet, she is covered. Occasionally, whenever she feels that she has made a point, she gives me a mischievous nudge with those beautiful toes. I don't mind at all. It feels good. I sit closer. The silver rings on her toes sparkle in the light and her anklets giggle at every move. Whenever she pauses in her narrative, she keeps admiring those pretty little feet that must have danced thousands of hours to bring her where she is today. I admire them too. They look like delicious slices of strawberry ice cream. She sees me looking at them and knows that she has won me over.

Zeenat was born in Bhopal in Madhya Pradesh to a family of traditional singers and dancers. They performed in the royal courts and were sought after to embellish ceremonies. With time and the fading away of royalty, they were at the mercy of big money. Dance soon gave way to other demands. Circumstances had changed and one had to adapt. Those were difficult days for women and for

Muslim women in particular,' says Zeenat. 'We were in purdah, we couldn't meet boys and we couldn't even go to school. We lived indoors and were being prepared for a life of servility. All that was expected of us was marriage and children, nothing else. It helped if we could cook. But I was talented and my father's pet. I was also rebellious. My father knew the dangers of encouraging his daughter. But he was an artiste and saw my talent and even fought with my mother to allow my talents to flourish. My mother was sad and happy for me. While she knew that I had it in me, she was scared that as a performing artiste I would see too much and then never fit in squarely anywhere. I would never ever belong completely. If I failed as a performer I would have nothing. A woman's role is that of a wife and mother. I would not have that either. Father saw that too. But he saw the desire to perform shining in my eyes and allowed me. Looking back, I must have given them so much pain. They are dead now. May Allah bless their souls.'

As Zeenat grew up, she sang and danced and even organized a travelling troupe. Men and women flocked to her shows. In the small towns of India, even today, women's emancipation is still a dream. They are consigned to bedrooms and kitchens and have no say in matters of consequence. Several decades ago, singing and dancing in front of men was worse than death. 'But I had the guts to go ahead,' says Zeenat. 'I had the ability and the will. I am very obstinate. If I fix my mind on something, I won't rest till it is mine. I defied conventions and I am proud of that.'

But Bhopal soon got too small for her and she started eyeing other options. A large travelling group of artistes passed by from Rajashtan and Zeenat joined them. They travelled all over India and Zeenat became its jewel. Her craft and beauty attracted attention. Her fame spread in the breeze of publicity. People came from all over to see her. She made money, catered to the remnants of royalty and had a large following. She did bit roles in films that were locally shot and then someone suggested that she move to

Mumbai to push her luck further. Zeenat had grown as a person and as a performer and couldn't be caged any longer in the small towns of India. 'I was a good dancer and singer. I was also ambitious. I decided to chance my destiny in Mumbai where everybody said I would strike gold. Anyway, even in Bhopal, I had struck out on my own. So I wasn't bothered about tongues wagging.' Mumbai is the living room of the Hindi film industry and all the stars she worked with asked her to come here and establish herself.

But Mumbai is a difficult city. It doesn't roll out the red carpet without checking out the newcomer. Zeenat had no place to stay. Mumbai has no time for stragglers and Zeenat was lonely and lost. She was a small-time girl peeking through the curtains at the glamour world. Mumbai is also an ocean of deceit and ambition. Talent is only one of the prerequisites for success in showbiz. Her family followed her and they moved often. She did a few film roles and several public appearances. There was some success despite the odds. But, most important, the freedom of the big city bit her hard and it was now difficult to go back to the closed mind of a small town. Mumbai had to be made home. Zeenat also travelled to different parts of the world doing stage shows as part of a group. She had arrived in an oblique way. She had her consorts; the rich and famous paraded their love for her. But time was running out and there was just that much she could do in addition to showing off her skills. She had her inhibitions and these did nothing to bolster her career.

'I keep getting offers even now,' she tells me. 'But this crazy lifestyle has affected my health. I sleep during the day and work at night. There are no fixed meal times. There is a lot of travel and it is difficult to cancel shows once they are arranged. I have had to perform even when I was very sick. I can't take all this any more. My body is getting stiff and my joints pain. I am not young anymore. But I still do special shows for special occasions. I also think that the hunger for fame is gone now. I just feel contented deep inside. I have done whatever I have wanted to. Now I only ask for His blessings and to forgive me for my sins. There is not much time left. For a beautiful woman, old age is a curse.'

Zeenat never married despite several romances and heartbreaks. It was part of the package of being gorgeous and well known. When it came to settling down with one man, she always backed off. 'They would get possessive and want to own me. I would have to listen to them. They didn't want me to work. And I didn't know if they wanted me or my fame and money. Men are unreliable. They court you, say beautiful words to get you, use you, and after that throw you away. They can never stick to one woman. I have been in love, too. I know the ecstasy and the pain. But I think the real reason I didn't marry was because I never wanted children. Now it is too late. I still get proposals and I ask the men why they want to marry an old woman.' She is filling her glass of whisky for the third time and offers me a large peg. We drink together.

She likes her drink and plays rummy in her spare time. She also trains young girls. Most of her earnings have been spent but there are a few wise investments and she is not badly off. 'Their parents have given them to me,' she says about her students. 'They live with me like my children and listen to whatever I tell them. I send them to school, arrange tutors and also teach them song and dance and take care of all their emotional and medical needs. It's been a fantastic life. I am not tired, because I think I have done whatever I wanted to. If some of these girls can carry on my art, it will be great.' I ask her if just singing and dancing supports all of them. What if there are other demands? She looks at me with clever eyes. 'You are an intelligent man. Come to your own conclusions.'

I watch the dances, and the men showering money and applause. There are regular customers and new ones brought in by middlemen. Women and men disappear together and new girls take their place. No one blinks an eye. It is happening in all the cubicles. Congress House is alive and well. Despite the crumbling walls, its soul is on fire. I share Zeenat's whisky. We empty the bottle. When the morning light falls on Congress House, it will be snoring in the slumber of spent passion.

If one speaks or acts with a cruel mind, misery follows, as the cart follows the horse... If one speaks or acts with a pure mind, happiness follows, as a shadow follows its source.

—The Dhammapada

The setting is ideal. Splintered from the regular drone of traffic and everyday bustle is a patch of green in the heart of Mumbai's commercial centre. Broken into driveways, manicured hedges and stretches of tightly clipped grass, it makes room in a corner for a handsome man and his even better-looking dream of imparting education to those born and brought up on the street.

The street is rough and without reins. Tethering young children who belong to it in a classroom is almost impossible. But Aijaz Ahmed, or Vada Pav Seth, as he is popularly called on the street, worked hard and made it happen. Certainly, an unusual call for an educated, sophisticated and softspoken gent from the more classy neighbourhoods of the city. Aijaz was an opening batsman in college, drove a fancy car and belonged to a Muslim family rich in old-world charm. His good looks and romantic air also had the ladies flocking to him.

How, then, did he make the street his workshop? It's a long story.

It wasn't easy and took years. Aijaz started out by getting to know the parents of the kids first. He got them gifts, tended to them when they fell sick and slowly, with time, like a miracle, the street took to him. Soon, he was walking around like the Pied Piper with the children in tow. Tall and slim, his grey hair fashionably cut, in his trademark white full-sleeved shirts and blue jeans with a bag slung over his shoulder, all Aijaz had to do was walk down the road and the street kids would follow him with joy in their hearts. He gave them pocket money, jobs when they needed them, got them school admissions, and paid for hospital expenses. Good students found homes in foreign countries, and those who stayed put in India on the street were equipped with the rare knowledge of math, English and good conduct. At least, they became better citizens.

Aijaz Ahmed gave the street hope.

Everyday, barring Saturday and Sunday, Aijaz would gather all the kids on the pavement and take them to the garden for their lessons. He bought the books, the crayons and the colours. He also allowed them to play football and cricket. The kids just loved it. Then, when it got late and the sun had set, they would return to their homes on the pavement to eat and sleep and dream of another day's cricket and colour.

'Please don't call me a social worker or activist,' he asks of me. 'I don't like those words. I don't want to be institutionalized. I am just doing this because I want to. I don't want money or fame or political recognition. When I feel my job is done, I will quietly slip away. As quietly as I wandered in.'

Aijaz lets me in to the details of this 'soul journey'. It was way back in 1978. He had seen the kids and wanted to help them, but it wasn't easy. He couldn't get a place to be with the children for a long time and had to keep relocating. The other big problem was to get to know the kids. They were born and brought up on the streets, and were more than just precocious. They grew up with drugs, gambling, street fights and the rage of hormones. They became parents early, and picked up several partners along the way as they grew up. How could they ever befriend a man so alien to their roots who offered them education, something they didn't understand and didn't need? The start was difficult.

'They kept seeing me and that helped,' says Aijaz. 'I used to sit in small cafes and have tea and biscuits. They got curious. We began talking. I got them tea and biscuits too. That broke the ice. That's how it all began. The parents wondered what I was up to. They thought I would kidnap the kids or lure them away. I had to get their trust, which was the most important.' The kids didn't know his name and weren't interested in it either but since he fed them Vada Pav, it was easy to call him Vada Pav Seth.

The boys outnumbered the girls and spent most of their free time watching films, doping, picking up quarrels and fighting in gangs or having sex. The pressures were so enormous that the children galloped into adulthood. 'The first thing I had to do,' says Aijaz, 'was to lure them away from begging. I had to give them self-worth, some self-pride. In all these years, they have never stolen a thing from me. If they wanted something, they asked me without hesitation, and when they earned money doing the odd job, they even bought their own crayons. Now many of them are working and their fathers borrow money from them. They have realized the value of work and that, I think, has been my greatest achievement. If they can work, they will never starve.'

Aijaz's success with street kids attracted worldwide attention. Several organizations involved in social work invited him to join their ranks. 'I don't want to make all this a business,' he says simply. 'A lot of money comes into all this from all over the world and disappears. Some people become rich and famous but the street kids remain on the street. I haven't come here for all that. I have brought hope into their lives and I am sure that they will grow into responsible adults. What more can one ask of them?'

The years passed. Aijaz did what he wanted to. He taught, looked after and guided a clutch of pavement kids. A new generation of pavement dwellers has now been added to the street. And like he always threatened to, Aijaz has disappeared into the hills. He lives a reclusive life reading, writing and painting the wilderness from a hilltop home.

Poverty is the parent of revolution and crime.
                                        —Aristotle

Dilip Kumar Sen is a coolie. Which only means that he is ready to do any work, however laborious. He says he is in his fifties, looks close to eighty, and is a refugee from East Bengal, now Bangladesh. His eyes are hollow, most of his teeth have fallen off, his face resembles a badly mowed lawn and old and tattered clothes hang limp on his broken spirit.

His bare legs are gnarled with thick veins that you suspect will burst any moment and spray you with fountains of blood. His flat feet are as large as flattened suitcases and his toes are crooked and overlapping one another. He has also lost two fingers of his left hand. He is ready to do anything, and I mean anything. His most profound quest in life has been the desire to eat a decent meal fairly regularly and he has not lost track of that quest in the vicissitudes of life.

I met him at the Victoria Terminus railway station, now renamed Chhatrapati Shivaji Maharaj station, in a fit of patriotism. But nothing else has changed. It is still dirty and is still known as VT.

Urchins, sex workers and the ubiquitous floater slip in and out throughout the day and night. The station also boasts a fairly substantial police presence. But millions of people use the local trains every day and you have to watch your wallet and your life with your third eye. Even that won't help, as Mumbai will testify.

'Can you give me a job?' he asks me. He smells like a municipal van that has carefully stored the city's refuse for a month. 'I just want to do anything. I need to eat something. I don't mind dying also. It is no use living like this.'

We go to one of the caterers on the platform and order food and tea for Sen. He gobbles it all and we order a refill. He tells me that he is a refugee from Pakistan. He came to India in 1951 from

Mymensingh, now in Bangladesh. There was an exodus from his village and they all landed up in different parts of India. 'We had land in Pakistan and a good life,' he continues. 'But there were Hindu-Muslim riots and we had to run away. We would have been killed. I didn't come here out of choice.'

They ran away from Pakistan and came to West Bengal. The borders are vast and porous. They travelled through Bihar, Assam and other states close to the border. His parents sent him to a local school. He studied for a few years and then dropped out. There was no money for more education. He then came to Mumbai looking for work. There was no place to stay and so he decided to live on Chowpatty beach because it was free.

'Life has always been very difficult,' he says. 'I had no money and once, when I came back from a dip in the sea, even my bag of clothes was missing. Somebody had stolen it. I had nothing left except the underwear I was wearing. Somehow, I managed to get a job with a building contractor carrying bricks and cement. That gave me some money and I could eat.'

He travelled to different states and worked at building sites, pulling carts, pushing heavy loads into lorries, anything he could get his hands on. As he got older and lost the strength to do hard labour, he became a professional blood donor. It was the easiest source of income for those who had no work. 'I grew very thin and kept falling sick,' he says. 'The doctors stopped accepting my blood. They said that my blood was not pure. Now I had no source of livelihood. I starved.'

He sold cigarettes and then worked as a helper in several shops. 'Nothing worked. My life has been miserable. This city is kind to some people and cruel to others. After all these years, I am still looking for food. Imagine. I have no clothes. I live on the pavement and when it rains I hide in the railway station. I used to sleep here before but now the police are very strict. I can't pay them. I have no money. I am no use to them. They don't even want me in jail. At least in jail I will get to sleep and eat. So they hit me and kick me out. I don't mind sitting in jail all my life if they allow me to.'

Sen will even forage garbage dumps, fighting with the strays for the best pieces of leftover food. The underworld has asked him many times to take to crime, do a few killings, smuggle goods across borders, and rob and maim. But he is scared. He doesn't have the guts or the brains for crime.

The meal is over. Sen asks for more food. He is ravenous. The station is forever crowded. Policemen, pimps, sex workers, pickpockets and petty thieves have taken up positions all along the pillars of this wonderful heritage building. They eye the swarming gentry, taking in every facial twitch, every shuffle, every pause, palpitation and confusion. Their antennae pick up even a whiff of fear. A newcomer to the city is easily noticed. Then they will swoop in for the kill.

The vulture is a patient bird. When the time is ripe, it will settle on carrion.

Joy is prayer – Joy is strength – Joy is love – Joy is a net of love by which you can catch souls.

—Mother Teresa

Noeline Delahunty is a social worker who has come to India to help out. She looks for a breather, sights a packet of cigarettes, makes a go for it and then changes her mind. She decides to pour herself another cup of tea instead. We are in the visitor's room at Asha Dan, the late Mother Teresa's hospice for the dying in central Mumbai. Graffiti screams across the walls, Bob Dylan is playing in the background and the laidback air of recess threatens to disturb the stark simplicity and rigid discipline of the home with its playful theme. Late afternoon sunlight streams in patterning the wall, the ceiling and the floor.

Noeline is in her late twenties. Tall and fair with golden-brown hair, she is in an off-white kurta pyjama. 'I am not used to interviews,' she warns me. 'In fact, I have never given one.' I tell her that I am not scared. Noeline is from Ireland. I ask her how, of all the places in the big, wide world, did she land up here? There are more people in a crowded Indian locality than there are in her country! She calmly tells me, 'It is the Lord's bidding. I got a call and had to come here.' The ring on the middle finger of her left hand, given by her mother for passing the school examinations, flashes brightly in the sunlight that is bouncing off the walls.

Noeline was born to a farmer in a quiet, lush green village in the Emerald Isle and was part of a large family of four brothers and seven sisters. 'It was a cushioned existence. I didn't step out till well past my adolescence.' She had heard of Mother Teresa and seen her on television. 'I had the usual life of an Irish schoolgirl with studies and socials but inside I knew I was always different.' She learnt nursing and took up a job at a private hospital in England. Then decided to chuck it all up and work for Mother Teresa. 'My family thought I was cracked.'

Noeline went to Nigeria. She drove ambulances and worked with doctors in the bush. 'It was lonely and very hard. The conditions were pathetic. I used to get homesick. All the time I was there I kept thinking of India. I don't know why but it was a recurring dream that had to materialize some day. I expected India to be thousands of times worse. But that didn't deter me one bit.'

She came to Kolkata in 1983. 'As soon as we touched DumDum airport, I wanted to return. It was in such a sorry state. I had prepared for the worst but it still shocked me. I went to the YWCA to stay and there was a power cut. What an introduction to India? I soon moved to an apartment and subsequently changed places many times.'

She began working the very next day and met Mother Teresa a few times. 'I had met her in Liverpool too before coming to

189

India,' she continues. 'I asked her about India and she told me, "Charity begins at home. Why do you want to come to India?" I was insistent. She finally said, "If God wants it, it will happen." I know that the lord wants me here.'

Kolkata, like Mumbai, but in a different way, has a way of getting you to like it. The people are warm and friendly and the soft flow of life is endearing despite all the difficulties. There is a fatalistic air that keeps the people relatively content. 'I soon fell in love with Kolkata,' says Noeline. 'I spent almost two years working in Nirmal Hriday (Tender Heart) and Prem Dan (Gift of Love). It was wonderful. The day began early. We used to bathe the patients, prepare their breakfast, give them medicines, wash and clean them as well as the surroundings. After lunch we did the dishes. It was so fulfilling.'

Noeline had visa problems in Kolkata and so 'Mother suggested that I go to Mumbai. The work here is the same but I enjoy it more because I live on the premises. I am on call all the time. I like to be useful. I am not the regular type of young woman. I feel and know that I am different. I am detached from the cycle of money, marriage, fame and ambition. This is all I ever asked for. It is Jesus who propels me. If not for him, I would have left long ago. India has glaring inequities and it is very frustrating. Nothing can be done about it. So I just work harder. My faith is blind and I don't question.'

Noeline has been working with the dying for long and is now used to seeing death up close. 'So many have died in my arms. It is so common here. I feel sad that they have suffered but happy that they have died here in the midst of so much love. I believe that life is temporary, a bridge to the next one.'

She hasn't been home for three years. They talk on the phone and write letters and the family is happy for her. Occasionally, she sees a film. She also enjoys folk and pop music and has got used to simple vegetarian food and a lifestyle without frills, like sleeping on the floor. 'I have seen the film *Gandhi* and am deeply influenced by his simplicity and love of non-violence.' There are several foreign volunteers from all over the world helping out. 'They all have their own reasons,' says Noeline. 'Who knows what has happened in whose life and from where and how the call has come? On a micro or macro level I have no plans. Every day is a new day. But given a choice I would like to do this all my life. The poor give me the greatest privilege of serving them. What greater miracle can I ask for?'